SAINTS ALIVE!

Scotland's Manager of the Year, Alex Totten.

SAINTS ALIVE!

Gordon Bannerman

Foreword by
ALEX TOTTEN
Manager of St Johnstone F.C.

SPORTSPRINT PUBLISHING

EDINBURGH

ISBN 0 85976 346 3

Phototypeset by Beccee Typesetting Services
Printed in Great Britain by Arrowsmith Limited, Bristol

Foreword

FOOTBALL has been my life since the day, as a raw 15-year-old, I joined Liverpool under the management of the legendary Bill Shankly and, without doubt, one of the proudest moments in a career spanning 30 years came when I was presented with Scotland's Tartan Special Manager of the Year award for 1991.

This recognition from the country's top sportswriters was the culmination of what must rank as the most exciting year in the history of St Johnstone. The award was not just for Alex Totten, but for everyone who had worked long and hard to bring soccer success to Perth.

All in all, it's been a remarkable five-year spell for the club under the guiding hand of chairman Geoff Brown and his fellow directors.

When I was appointed manager of this club the number one priority was to escape the clutches of the Second Division. At the time I recall telling supporters I could make them no promises, but they were assured of 100 per cent effort as we strove to bring them success.

Players have come and players have gone in the four years I've been at Perth and they've all played their part in transforming the on-field fortunes of the club.

In all my years in football, I doubt if I have ever encountered a club more richly endowed with team spirit and harmony. It's apparent way beyond the confines of the dressing room, encompassing every apsect of the impressive set-up at McDiarmid Park.

In this book, journalist Gordon Bannerman provides a glimpse behind the scenes of a football club re-born in the last five years, through the eyes of the board, management and players responsible for marching The Saints back to a position of prominence in Scottish football.

Alex Totten,
Scotland's Manager of the Year

Acknowledgements

The author would like to thank the directors, management and staff of St Johnstone Football Club — past and present — for their co-operation in the preparation of this book. Further thanks are extended to understanding colleagues on the *Perthshire Advertiser*.

All black and white photographs courtesy of the *Perthshire Advertiser*. Thanks to Pam Bird, Graeme Lafferty, David Wallace and Richard Wilkins, Graham Fulton and Paul Smith.

Colour photograph of McDiarmid Park courtesy of Vince Chapman Studios, Dewsbury.

Colour cover photograph of Alex Totten courtesy of Harry Goodwin, Chorlton-cum-Hardy, Manchester.

Colour action cover photograph courtesy of Sportapic Sports Agency, Glasgow.

Photograph of Willie Ormond courtesy of Louis Flood Photographers, Perth.

Contents

The Story of the Blues

GUESTS arriving at the Stakis Dunblane Hydro on the night of November 26, 1989, to celebrate the Centenary of St Johnstone Football Club were late. Five years late.

The Perth club can trace roots back to 1884 and official membership of the Perthshire Association was duly logged the following year. But sadly, entry to Scotland's elite 100 Club coincided with a less than vintage year, as fortunes on and off the field impressed neither fan nor accountant.

Ejection from the Premier League had been followed by a season of abject misery for the contracting Perth support. By the late spring of 1985, the ailing Centenarian was ready to drop. Division Two engagements beckoned and the credit rating was on par with the dismal league placing.

The party atmosphere was missing from Muirton Park. A club created by Fair City cricketers had reached the century mark, but it was a close run thing. With the bank manager following results more closely than the public at large, it had been dispatched to the far pavilions of Scottish football. Not surprisingly, the mood was sombre, rather than celebratory.

In two turbulent seasons, the Saints found themselves ex-communicated from the broad church offered by the Premier League and the First Division. There were many among the suffering supporters who feared they hadn't a prayer of returning to the fold.

Yet within the space of five extraordinarily, exciting years, the Perth club has been resurrected. The exploits last season at the highest level of Scottish football surpassed all expectation and Saints can lay claim to a purpose-built stadium which is the envy of clubs the length and breadth of Britain.

McDiarmid Park is the third home occupied by the Perth club. Muirton Park had witnessed the magnificent, the mundane and the downright mournful before being pensioned off — fittingly at the age of 65 — on April 29, 1989. But the story of this football club really begins one autumn evening in 1884.

Members of the St Johnstone Cricket Club, their practice over, reportedly 'indulged in promiscuous kicking' as dusk fell. A perfectly innocent diversion it transpires, and within weeks John Colborn, as captain, and William Imrie, as secretary, had fixed up a game with one of the existing local sides.

The cricket chaps, sporting black and white, beat the Hibernians by a single goal and expressed themselves 'well pleased' with their efforts. Other bounce games followed against Caledonian, Fair City, Pullar's Rangers and a return with Hibernians before the start of the new cricket season.

The Perthshire Constitutional of the period reported that more mature elements of the populace were disenchanted with 'the incessant playing of football' on the public Inches. Damaging the turf it was. Neither were golfers and cricketers escaping the flak. After all, this sporting life was interfering with the serious business of dyeing and bleaching of clothes. But come August 15, 1885, the dour citizens of Perth had no cause to cast complaints in the direction of St Johnstone Football Club. The Saints had secured a home of their own.

No doubt many sons of the toil and soil had succumbed to the lure of the brave new world adverts of the period. How many pondered a slice of prime prairie land in South West Minnesota, modestly touted by the America Land and Colonization Company of Scotland as 'the most fertile soil in the American continent,' and how many parted with £7 for the privilege of sailing to Queensland in class? Albeit third class.

But unlike certain of their contemporaries, city cutler George Valentine and young solicitor Duncan McNab (later a Lord Provost of Perth) were concerned with matters closer to home. With £20 accrued by £1 per head subscriptions, they secured the lease on land at Craigie Haugh from Sir Robert Moncreiffe.

Situated opposite Perth Prison, the land was levelled and drained. A wooden barrier was erected around the playing surface and the club acquired a grandstand which had once graced Perth

Ormond's Muirton Aces.

Hunt Race meetings at the North Inch. St Johnstone Football Club was alive and kicking.

The Recreation Ground, as it became known, was to serve the Saints until admission to the First Division came their way in 1924. But the Perth club was posted missing from the official opening match on August 15, 1885. They let Queen's Park, then big box office, and Dundee Our Boys (later to become Dundee Football Club) do the honours.

'Perth folk,' recorded local historian and one-time player, Peter Baxter some years later, 'wended their way in hundreds to see the new game that was more exciting that cricket.' The Glasgow amateurs duly dished up goals galore, to dismiss the Our Boys challenge 6-1. Any elation en route back to Glasgow was as nothing compared with that experienced by hosts gathering up gate receipts of £50. A nice little earner indeed.

But St Johnstone's early on-field fortunes were slow to build. After a spell draped in black and white, followed by maroon, blazoned with a striking white shield, the team adopted blue and white. And in 1989, the first silverware, in the shape of The Perthshire Cup, came their way.

By 1907 they were taking the first tentative steps towards professionalism. The traditionalists were horrified. But the lure of the filthy lucre, in the form of 'travel expenses,' attracted the best of local talent, given the option of values Corinthian and capitalist. Within three years, the club had opted for limited company status.

Before the Kaiser intervened with a time-out, Saints were savouring a small measure of success. Their first 'national triumph' — the Scottish Consolation Cup at the expense of Dumbarton at Ibrox — had the team hailed as local heroes in 1911. But come the end of the Great War, the Perth club found themselves frozen out of the Central League. Only silver-tongued diplomacy and energetic lobbying ensured the resumption of normal service.

St Johnstone have scaled the heights, but rarely, since their inception. All too often the glory trail has run cold or led expectant fans up a cul de sac. On occasion, the light at the end of the tunnel has indeed proved to be a train, as on March 31, 1934.

Hampden Park welcomed more than 60,000 that day, to see if the Perth provincials could derail a Rangers team en route to a league and cup double. In short, they could not. A single goal saw to that. But this was a tantalising taste of the good life.

By now, Saints were operating from Muirton Park. A £10,000 debenture and the largesse of local landowner Lord Mansfield paved the way for an official opening by Lord Provost, the Hon. John Dewar, on Christmas Day, 1924. Queen's Park — old hands at the game — were welcomed back, but on this occasion St Johnstone had a part in the proceedings. The league points stayed in Perth with a 2-1 scoreline and 12,000 observers on hand for the occasion.

Saints were part of the big picture, if only just. The First Division beckoned in 1923. But the welcome mat was whipped abruptly from beneath their feet by the League Management committee, ruling that the Perth club had breached the transfer deadline. A £20 fine and the loss of two points brought forth much wailing and gnashing of teeth, but little in the way of comfort.

Clydebank, when found guilty of a similar contravention, had escaped with a £100 fine and no purloining of the points. It was enough to hoist them into Division One. But the following

Alex Rennie's 1983 Division One champions.

season, the clubs exchanged working environments, raising spirits (doubtless by the glass) in the Fair City.

Press notes of the period reported: 'Never in the history of Perth football have such scenes been witnessed as those which took place on the return of St Johnstone directors and several of the players from Armadale. The news of Saints' fine victory, which assured them of the Second Division League championship and the coveted gold badges, quickly flashed throughout the city, and thousands of people gathered at Perth General Station to await the arrival of the special train.

'Rousing cheers rent the air as the special steamed into the station, and very soon McRoberts, Walker, Fleming and Wilson were seen towering above the masses. Hardly had they left their carriages ere they were shouldered by the excited crowd.'

The heroes were carried shoulder high from the station to the County Hotel, where it was noted, several thousand fans burst into song. 'For He's A Jolly Good Fellow,' they chorused, with their pin-up player Fleming responding: 'Good old St Johnstone.' Times, and the tunes, have changed a touch in the intervening years.

Hit man John Brogan shows the 'goal-den' touch.

From the hotel window, club president Robert Campbell announced: 'Ladies and gentlemen, on behalf of the St Johnstone players I want to thank you for your local reception of the team tonight. The players have worthily upheld the reputation of Perth as a sporting centre and next year they will just as worthily uphold it in the First League.'

Before the outbreak of the Second World War, St Johnstone enjoyed First Division status. At the close of hostilities in Europe, they did not. New 'A' and 'B' divisions were introduced and Saints didn't care for this alphabet game. Slotted into the second grade, it was clear they were bit players in the power-broking game.

The Fifties unfolded, bringing Dundee and a 29,972 crowd to Muirton for a Scottish Cup tie on February 10, 1952. That was about all the decade brought to Perth. But, under Bobby Brown and Willie Ormond, both serving apprenticeships for the Scotland national team, the Sixties were positively swinging.

In 1960, the Second Division championship flag fluttered over Muirton, with Saints returning to the top after an absence of 21 years. The yo-yo effect brought relegation and promotion in succeeding years. Throughout the decade, Perth continued to fulfil its time-honoured role as a breeding ground for emerging talent. In November 1968, for instance, promising midfielder Alex MacDonald departed in an exchange deal: Saints exchanging the player's services for a £50,000 cheque from Rangers.

Doing what comes naturally: Ally McCoist opens his account against Celtic in 1981.

The previous year, on March 24, 1967, one William Ormond was enticed to the managerial post at Muirton Park. Further down the line, an OBE was to come his way. Had Saints supporters had their say, he'd have received the keys of Buckingham Palace to accompany it.

Cynics will say Willie Ormond won nothing during his six year tenure of office. A Scottish Cup semi-final (taken to a replay), League Cup disappointment at the final and semi-final stage, third place in the League and three European ties at Muirton Park: those are the cold statistics. But this remarkable wee man won the undying affection of a generation of Perth football fans.

In his first season at the helm, he navigated the club to a League Cup semi-final, losing 3-1 to traditional rivals Dundee. But the learning process continued. On October 25, 1969, the A9 south to Glasgow was a cavalcade of blue and white. Perth, and much of the surrounding area, was decanting to Hampden Park, in the company of Donaldson, Lambie, Coburn; Gordon, Rooney, McPhee; Aird, Hall, McCarry, Connolly, Aitken. Twelfth man: Whitelaw. Celebrated Perth bard Willie Soutar surely never penned sweeter poetry. They returned without the League Cup. Celtic, courtesy of an early Bertie Auld goal, saw to that. But this was the stuff of dreams.

Top table guests at the belated Centenary Dinner.

At the close of season 1970-71, St Johnstone proudly occupied third place. A perch so lofty, and unprecedented, that players might have been forgiven a touch of vertigo. They won 19 of 34 league games, amassing 44 points, with Henry Hall tallying 20 goals all-in. The elegant John Connolly, another all-time terracing favourite, struck with 18.

The season bowed out at Muirton with an insipid scoreless draw against Morton on March 24. Come April 12, St Johnstone were gracing Real Madrid's breathtaking Bernabeu Stadium, surrendering the friendly 3-1. But, as those of a nostalgic disposition would remind us, with nine minutes left the honours were even.

This was unknown territory for the Perth club. But Saints had the passports looked out again in September for a sojourn to Hamburg. This was the real thing, the UEFA Cup, and the cynics scoffed they'd have more chance of scoring were they to pass on the football and go window shopping in the red light district. But they bid Auf Wiedersehen to Gemany, losing 2-1 to the celebrated SV side. Jim Pearson scored on foreign soil, to be joined at Perth by Hall and Gordon Whitelaw, as Saints went marching on in style. Nearly 12,000 eye-witnesses could verify the astounding 3-0 scoreline.

Vasas of Budapest were next to the sword after a two-goal win in Perth — Connolly and Pearson — and a single goal defeat in

Familiar faces: members of Willie Ormond's side at the Centenary event.

Hungary, where that gloriously eccentric keeper Jimmy Donaldson saved a penalty kick. Next up were Zeljeznicar Sarajevo: a big name in Yugoslavia, and quite a mouthful in English. By this time, more than a few celebrated sides were taking note of Saints progress, and scrutinising the map of Scotland for this place called St Johnstone.

At Muirton, a Connolly strike was meagre reward for 90 minutes of incessant pressure but, once again, the Perth club had shut out the fancied continentals. Not surprisingly, the party travelled in confidence.

But Sarajevo, infamous for the shots which accounted for Archduke Franz Ferdinand to trigger the First World War, proved the graveyard of St Johnstone's first European campaign. The home side hit five, with Benny Rooney replying for a muted Saints. But the defeat was overshadowed by near-disaster on the runway, when an ice-clad plane flirted alarmingly with the tree tops. The passports went back in the drawer and there they have remained.

The Ormond Era drew to a close in 1973 when Scotland's recruitment policy again relieved St Johnstone of a manager, as the powers-that-be sought a successor to Tommy Docherty. Not a few misty-eyed supporters feared they would not see the like again.

The man charged with filling the vacuum created by Ormond's departure was Dumbarton boss Jackie Stewart. The outlook was bright as Saints secured membership of the new Premier League elite in 1975, with a Scottish football product repackaged to lure back the paying customer. This was to be the bright, new dawn. Alas, it proved all too false for the Fair City club.

St Johnstone's ejection from the upper echelons was rubber stamped in April. But, in truth, the issue had been settled long before. Victory over Dundee United at Perth on the opening day of the league season — a derby attracting only 3,300 fans — provided the players with one of only three win bonuses to come their way in a miserable season.

Eleven points from 36 fixtures, a barren away win column and a 27-match run without collecting the two points on offer prompted the resignation of Jackie Stewart before the official coup de grace. Jim Storrie arrived clutching a managerial curriculum vitae limited to English non league side Waterlooville, and only a 4-1 win at Dumfries warded off the threat of a relegation double for players now operating on a part-time basis. Lady Luck was to be less kindly disposed towards the Saints at a later date.

Alex Stuart came and went before 1980 saw the return of former club captain Alex Rennie as tracksuit manager. A refreshing air of optimism was detectable down the Dunkeld Road way and on February 14 of the following year, Muirton Park was to witness one of its more dramatic moments.

Rangers came to town on Scottish Cup business, found a two-goal lead overhauled and, with only seconds remaining, they faced the door marked exit — until Errol-born Ian Redford conjured up an act of escapology unprecedented since the heyday of Harry Houdini. A certain Ally McCoist scored at Ibrox but the replay was a formality at 3-1. If only . . .

Promotion was put on hold until 1982-83. A tense draw at Alloa witnessed by around 3,000 fans secured the all-important step-up and, appropriately, striker John Brogan clinched the title against Dunfermline with one of his record 140 goals for St Johnstone. In eight years with the Saints, Brogan beat the previous 116 club scoring record set by Ian Rodger in the fifties.

Willie Ormond

The five he notched in a 1982 League Cup tie against Falkirk equalled Rodger's individual total for one game away from home. Neither striker, however prolific, could match the six scored by Willie McIntosh at Muirton on March 9, 1946, in a 9-0 win over Albion Rovers.

But once again, the Perth side proved ill-equipped to survive the rigours of the Premier League. They slid out of the reckoning in ninth place . . . and the momentum carried them ever deeper into the mire. The First Division stay was brief and again Saints succumbed to that sinking feeling.

With club finances dipping alarmingly — a simple glance around decaying Muirton Park bore ample testimony to a balance sheet which refused steadfastly to live up to its name — midfield player Ian Gibson was offered a 12-month, part-time contract in the summer of 1985.

At 29, the youngest manager in Scottish football was charged with the daunting task of reviving an ailing Centenarian, burdened by the knowledge that the life support machine was running on empty. The prognosis for St Johnstone Football Club made grim reading, and the obituaries were being prepared.

Laying the Foundations

AS the story goes, it was one Patrick Cobbald, as chairman of Ipswich Town, who was asked what might constitute a crisis at the East Anglian club. 'Well,' he replied, after giving the matter due consideration, 'If we ran out of white wine in the boardroom.'

Sadly, by the summer of 1986, the troubled directors of St Johnstone Football Club had more pressing matters to occupy their attention than the state of the Muirton Park drinks cabinet.

On the footballing front, Saints had gone where no other had gone before, from the Premier League's star-spangled galaxy to soccer's equivalent of the Black Hole — the Second Division — in consecutive seasons. Ian Gibson, who had moved from the transfer list to the managerial office in June, 1985, was left to trawl the Tayside amateur and junior leagues to bolster his squad. And only 27,000 fans had troubled to turn out for 23 home matches, as Saints posted results which equalled their worst since the war.

The Dunkeld Road stadium, where youngsters now enjoyed free rein to play 'shootie-in' during half-time breaks, was falling apart at the seams. Had it been of an earlier vintage, it might have attracted the attention of the Historic Buildings and Monuments experts. Instead, only those charged with responsibilities under the Safety at Sports Grounds Act interested themselves in a decaying relic from the Twenties.

En route to sixth place in the Division Two final listings, the fans had deserted in droves. By the turn of the year, the Muirton Park terracing provided the ideal afternoon retreat for anyone prone to claustrophobia.

It was against this depressingly bleak background that the call came through to Geoff Brown, a local businessman for whom the self-made-man mantle might have been tailored. Would he care to take-in the final match of the season as a guest of the Perth board? the caller ventured.

'The idea was to meet the directors. But there were so few fans in the ground to see Saints share two goals with Queen of the South that I could have introduced myself to each and every one of them quite easily,' recalled Brown. Had he been there the month before — on April 19 to be precise — he would have shared the company of a meagre 466 customers for the visit of Albion Rovers.

The board, it transpired, was seeking to bring in new blood. The recruitment drive was to centre on businessmen with enterprise, and a bob or two, prepared to throw the club a lifeline.

'It quickly became clear that this was a club with serious problems. At the time, I didn't know the full extent of the crisis, but it didn't take a genius to appreciate the effects of two disastrous seasons since relegation from the Premier League,' said Brown.

'For a start, it was obvious there would be no football at all at Muirton come August unless the club finally implemented safety measures demanded by Tayside Regional Council. But where was the money to come from? The only sign of income on the horizon was the first home match of the season — how was the club to survive until then? There was nothing to suggest the directors could find the money needed to ensure football at Muirton Park.'

Expenses had been trimmed. The manager's phone had gone the way of the team bus booking. The weekly meetings in the wood-panelled boardroom were dominated by discussions of bills old and new. Those marked 'Final Reminder' or accompanied by a lawyer's letter enjoyed precedence.

Brown explained: 'They had borrowed up to their limit at the bank. Every one of the directors had done as much as he could, but they really didn't know where to turn. They had run out of ideas. That can happen to anyone.'

After more than 16 years as his own boss — the one-time local joiner had built up an extensive business empire founded on house-building — he was reluctant to be sucked into a 'decisions by committee' scenario.

'People might say I'm a bit of a tyrant at times, but I firmly believe no business can run successfully without a firm hand on the helm,' Brown insisted. 'At the time, I made a statement which might have been taken the wrong way. With hindsight, I might have phrased it more delicately! But the gist of it was that St Johnstone needed Geoff Brown more than Geoff Brown needed them.

'That might sound arrogant to some and I'm sure the directors didn't like it. But it was the truth. Had I been approached to become a club director four years previously I would have seen it as a great honour and a privilege. After all, Saints have always been my local team.

'I used to go to Muirton with my father in the Fifties and I remember joining a pal from Perth High School on the terracings — shaking a collecting can for the pipe band which once played at every home game. As the eldest of six children of a market gardener, money was pretty tight. That was the only way to see the football without paying!

'But by the time this invitation was extended, the club had reached rock bottom. They were clutching at straws. They needed an immediate injection of capital and some fresh ideas. Anyone who thinks this was an ego-trip for Geoff Brown should remember I didn't chase St Johnstone Football Club. It was about football — something that's always been close to my heart — and it was about Perth. Had there been any other takers, they could have had the club. Given the state it was in, I wouldn't have fought them for it.'

Born and bred in the Fair City area, Brown was adamant that no other challenge would have kindled his interest. A previous approach from a Tayside club — then in better shape financially — was rebuffed politely, but firmly.

Initially the St Johnstone directors were looking to secure the services of someone capable of baling out a sinking ship and staying aboard to stoke the boiler. Many weeks passed before they were to relent and surrender control of the bridge.

'I told them I wasn't prepared to join on their terms, but I offered to act as a consultant to help with the ground problems. I was only interested in closer involvement if the directors gave the go-ahead for a £150,000 rights issue — and agreed not to take their entitlement, ensuring the money remained within the club. That was left on the table over the summer.'

Boardroom shuffle: Geoff Brown and Alex Lamond (front), with Allan Campbell, Angus Baillie, David Sidey and Henry Ritchie.

The club survived to see the opening of the 1986/87 season but a 5-1 opening day defeat from Meadowbank set the alarm bells clamouring again. A home defeat by Albion Rovers on August 26 was followed by an official club announcement of a major boardroom shake-up.

Brown was to become managing director, with a hand-picked team in tandem. The club was anchored at the foot of the Second Division with debts approaching £275,000 and weekly losses of £3,500 simply keeping pace with interest payments. There were some, among outsiders, who suggested a wand, rather than a wallet, was going to be required.

Before the rights issue and boardroom package could be approved at an extraordinary shareholders' meeting arranged for Muirton Park on September 23, innumerable discussions took place beteween the Muirton heir apparent and local blue bloods. Between them, sleeping shareholders Lord Mansfield and Lord Forteviot controlled 26 per cent of the club — a historic link dating back to the debentures and land which created Muirton Park.

Natural concern for the future of the football club in the hands of a major property developer was put in perspective by the stark realities of the club's calamitous condition: 'It's 13 per cent of nothing or four per cent of something.' Within days, the projected rights issue was given the aristocratic seal of approval.

A £100,000 loan from G.S. Brown Construction and a further £50,000 injected personally by the managing director restored the club to a trading position, however precarious. The transformation had begun.

The M.D. head-hunted the men he wanted to kick-start the Perth club into action. It would hardly have done to advertise in the situations vacant columns. Just imagine: 'Wanted. Directors with fresh ideas, unbounded enthusiasm, limitless commitment — and willing to work all the hours, free gratis! Apply Muirton Park.' How many takers would there have been?

'I've always felt a senior football club should be part of the community. It's part of our heritage. And to revive St Johnstone, well-known local businessmen Allan Campbell, Henry Ritchie and David Sidey were brought onto the board,' said Geoff. 'Each had a specific role to play. And the success of this club in subsequent years can be attributed directly to the many people who have committed themselves voluntarily to St Johnstone. I can't even begin to guess at the incredible time and effort these individuals have devoted to this club.'

Marketing expertise had been negligible at Muirton Park. Only one of the peeling, advertising hoardings bordering the playing surface had been rented, for the princely sum of £100. The rest were but sad and mocking reminders of better days. It was Allan Campbell's daunting brief to stir enthusiasm, and hard cash, from the business community he knew as director with Fair City Amusements.

Henry Ritchie, a co-director of G.S. Brown Construction, was charged with special responsibility for restoring Muirton Park to the satisfaction of authorities which had imposed a 2,500 crowd limit. His qualifications for the task were unimpeachable — and he was a self-confessed Saints fanatic.

Glazing firm boss David Sidey, although plagued by ill-health, was well-known on the local soccer scene and his primary role was to be public relations. For the first time in years, a director was to offer a high profile at reserve fixtures, specifically welcoming young trialists and their parents to the Perth club.

Later, Perth electrical contractor Douglas McIntyre was drafted

Alex Totten, St Johnstone's 13th manager, flanked by assistant Bertie Paton and chairman Geoff Brown.

in to bolster the board, playing a crucial role in the development of McDiarmid Park as St Johnstone moved into territory beyond the grasp of even the most imaginative supporter. In 1990, Stewart Duff, a banker, one-time junior football administrator, and veteran of Saints' travels to Hamburg, was co-opted to the McDiarmid board in recognition of his sterling secretarial and general management duties.

This was to be no bloodless revolution. Among the first casualties were the club's sports shop (antiquated stock with a paper value of £60,000 was knocked down at a tenth in the clear out). The lottery went the same way and the first transfer was the club bank account!

Before the year was out, solicitor Alex Lamond, chairman since 1977, and Angus Baillie had both resigned, following the way of Lindsay Dow and the late Dr Eric Mathieson who intimated their resignations during the close season. For a brief period, long-serving club secretary, George Bell, was to take a seat at board meetings.

The rights issue was launched with a view to G.S. Brown Construction taking up 56 per cent of the £1 shares. After examining the tax implications, Brown acquired that allotment in person. Supporters and well-wishers responding in the club's hour of need applied for around 20,000 units, allowing the heart to rule the head. As investment opportunities went, it could hardly be regarded in the Blue Chip bracket.

Even the newly installed managing director cautioned it could be some time before any dividend emerged on the football front. In a *Perthshire Advertiser* interview within days of taking control, he stated: 'The Premier League is not a realistic prospect in the short-term. We have to get the wagon rolling. But I genuinely believe St Johnstone should be quoted in Scotland's top 12 clubs.'

On-field, Saints began their second season in Division Two in faltering fashion. Ian Gibson, elevated to combine labours in the midfield with the managerial office when still short of his 29th birthday, was contracted until the end of the season. In fact, the parting of the ways came after a two goal defeat at Perth by Queens Park on April 11, 1987.

That result dispelled any lingering notion that Saints could figure in the frame for promotion. Gibson inquired if his part-time contract was to be renewed, got the answer he, presumably, expected and duly announced to the media that he had been sacked. Physiotherapist Jim Peacock was re-acquainted with a previous role as stand-in boss.

'Appointing Ian Gibson as player manager was an easy option for the previous board. They left themselves wide open to criticism for that cop-out,' maintained Brown. 'It's all very well appointing respected players like Graeme Souness and Kenny Dalglish to the managerial role. But look at the back-up they enjoyed in the initial phase. Gibson had no money, and no experienced backing. He faced an impossible task.'

The manager certainly didn't have his troubles to seek, with assistant manager Derek Addison — a record buy four years previously — turning his back on the club before the season started. Then there was the small matter of that 5-1 thrashing from Meadowbank — and a player pool restricted to 16.

Premier League Clydebank cruised through a Skol Cup tie by three goals — Saints never looked likely to secure a win bonus of £300 per player, with a similar sum on offer for each and every goal. After the infamous Albion Rovers humiliation, Gibson confessed: 'Unless cash is forthcoming we will never get out of the Second Division.'

But the new spirit of optimism injected by the boardroom

changes percolated through to the manager. Before the turn of the year, Gibson expressed the conviction that promotion was back on the agenda. Saints, bolstered by recruits including fragile winger and player coach Graeme Payne (who had featured in Scotland's 40-strong 1978 World Cup pool) were a single point off the pace.

But that pace proved too much in March and, after what proved to be his final game in charge, Ian Gibson revealed: 'I feel for the supporters of St Johnstone Football Club. They will give me stick but, deep down, I know that they deserve better than they have had over the last four weeks.'

Brown maintained: 'He simply didn't have the managerial capability a club like St Johnstone required, given its troubled position in both the playing and financial sense.

'Players came in that season, despite the financial predicament. For instance, we brought Don McVicar back to Perth for the princely sum of £600. There were a couple of other buys, but when Ian Heddle arrived from Dunfermline that involved £3,500, after protracted negotiations. Big money in those days I can assure you!'

With the manager's post vacant, who was to be responsible for pinpointing the escape route from Second Division obscurity? By this stage, Saints new dream home was still at the drawing board stage. But the potential was to be a major selling point working in St Johnstone's favour.

Three candidates were under consideration but the directors raised their sights beyond the Muirton postbag. They went head-hunting and were pleasantly surprised when it emerged that Alex Totten, always a firm favourite in the media guessing game, was not under contract at Dumbarton. Saints played it by the book, approaching the late Sir Hugh Fraser for permission to speak to his manager, and the Avonside Homes offices at Castlecary provided the venue for one of the most telling days in St Johnstone history.

On April 27, 1987, Alex Totten was introduced to the Press as the new manager of St Johnstone, with assistant Bertie Paton at his side. His first match in charge, with Raith Rovers sharing the points in the season's swansong, stirred the Perth public from its slumbers. More than 1,700 clicked through the turnstiles, hinting at the potential support which might one day be harnessed.

'Alex Totten's decision to come to Perth surprised a lot of people. He had taken Dumbarton to the brink of promotion to the Premier League, yet here he was dropping down into the Second Division,' said his new chairman. 'More than a few were asking how a club like Saints had managed to attract a manager of this calibre and proven ability.

'Despite his success with Dumbarton, crowds were less than 1,000. He recognised the potential at St Johnstone. Planning permission had been received for the new stadium and that must have played a major part in his decision.

'We saw Alex Totten as a man with a proven track record. He had been successful at Falkirk and Alloa, with a reputation for playing positive, attacking football. The only question was whether he had been demoralised, or his enthusiasm diminished, by the experience at Ibrox, when his assistant managerial job went with the arrival of Graeme Souness.

'We felt his experience at that level of the game could work to our advantage. St Johnstone didn't have cash, but we promised that any money generated would be made available to strengthen the team. Alex Totten had a close knowledge of players at every level of Scottish senior football and we wanted to cash in on that.

'But above all, we saw Alex Totten as the ideal ambassador for the club. He enjoys enormous respect. Alex is described often as a "player's manager" but, above all, he is a gentleman. He was perfect for the image we wanted this football club to convey.'

Only seven months after the composition of the new-look board received the blessing of St Johnstone shareholders, the fans at last had due cause for optimism. The foundations had been laid and now the serious building work could begin.

Emerging from the Shadows

IT was 4 p.m. precisely, on November 18, 1983, as Alex Totten strode up the wood-panelled Marble Staircase dominated by the broad canvas of Alan Morton, the celebrated 'Wee Blue Devil' of Ibrox. Glasgow Rangers Football Club had a new assistant manager on the payroll.

That evening, as manager Jock Wallace introduced his colleague to club directors, a blueprint for continuity down Edmiston Drive was unveiled to the latest recruit. Totten, it transpired, was to be groomed as the next occupant of the managerial office.

On April 7, 1986, Jock Wallace found his second contract with Glasgow Rangers terminated, as chairman David Holmes engineered the dramatic introduction of Graeme Souness to Scottish football. Seven days later, a trio of backroom staff were summoned upstairs.

'Our services were no longer wanted, and it didn't come as a surprise,' recalled Alex Totten. 'I was recognised as Jock's right-hand man and, naturally, Graeme Souness wanted to have his own team around him. I went back to clear my desk and left a note wishing Walter Smith — a man I'd always respected — the very best of luck.

'Before leaving the stadium I visited Graeme Souness in the manager's office, just to say there were no hard feelings and to wish him well. I meant every word. Football management is a precarious line to be in and there was no point being bitter.'

Totten shared in two League Cup final triumphs, with victories over Celtic and Dundee United: 'Sure, leaving Ibrox was a kick in the teeth at the time — but the experience has stood me in good stead. Turning my back on football never entered my head. I've loved the game ever since the days when, as a kid, I'd get a new strip, boots and tin of dubbin at Christmas.'

Boghead, Dumbarton, isn't so very far from Ibrox, Glasgow . . . if measured in miles. In terms of finance, glamour and surroundings, the two could be on different planets. But Totten tackled this assignment with the enthusiasm and commitment which has hallmarked his managerial career.

By the time St Johnstone expressed an interest, Dumbarton had been propelled to third place in the First Division. Promotion may have been a future possibility, but Totten fast came to the conclusion that it would be easier hoisting the famous town Rock onto his shoulders than nudging attendance figures past a thousand.

After being appointed the 13th manager of St Johnstone Football Club, he explained: 'Lots of people might think it's a step back to leave the First Division but I don't see it that way. This is a new era for St Johnstone, with new directors, new management and a new stadium coming up. We are all ambitious for this club.'

Division Two was a familiar part of the football world for Totten. During a spell at Alloa, before further success with Falkirk, he had charted the club's progress from 38th position in the Scottish league structure to the more respectable elevation of the First Division. Saints were hoping to pursue the same route.

When chairman Geoff Brown and director Allan Campbell presented the St Johnstone sales pitch to the new boss it was made clear money would be made available, if and when it was generated. Totten was quick to see the potential at Perth: 'In my playing days Saints were regarded as a big club in Scotland and the directors convinced me they could be once again.

'The possibility of a new stadium didn't really come into it. At Dumbarton, Ibrox and Parkhead were just across the Erskine Bridge and crowds rarely left the 750-800 bracket. I knew it would be different at Perth if the club was doing well. As it turned out, my decision to take one step backwards was quickly vindicated — Saints and Dumbarton were to pass each other at the end of the season.'

The Perth chairman dispensed with the diplomatic niceties when asked to rate the squad inherited by the new manager: 'The standard of player generally was at an all-time low. It was one of the worst teams St Johnstone had ever had. It was a disgrace that some of these players ever got to the stage of pulling a senior shirt over their heads.'

As the season petered out, Totten's first act was to extend a 'Meet the Manager' invitation to the fans. The upshot was an immediate rapport with the support. As befits a master of public relations, a blue and white scarf had been acquired — but the fans pressed ahead regardless with a 'personalised' number for the new season!

The one chance of casting an eye over his inheritance was presented by a 1-1 draw, when Raith Rovers visited Perth for the final match of the season: 'I organised two trial games to sort out the wheat from the chaff — and then freed 11 players. Things weren't happening at Muirton, otherwise I wouldn't have been offered the job. I couldn't see any potential and they weren't good enough for Alex Totten. As it turned out, only Gordon Winter at Forfar survived in senior football, and even he had a spell back in the junior ranks.

'I knew I had a job on my hands before the season kicked-off in August, but there were encouraging signs. The fans, for instance, responded. I told them I couldn't make any promises. The only thing I could guarantee was 100 per cent effort and honest endeavour.

'Obviously, my ultimate aim was the Premier Division. That's what football is all about — pitting yourself against the very best. That holds true whether you're a manager or a player. We wanted to get there as quickly as possible. But the first priority was to lift St Johnstone out of the Second Division and I knew it wouldn't be easy.'

Totten came to Perth accompanied by assistant boss Bertie Paton, an experienced player with Dunfermline in their European heyday and a past manager in his own right with Cowdenbeath and Raith Rovers. There was also a coaching spell under Willie Ormond at Hearts.

'We worked well together at Dumbarton and I had no hesitation in asking him to join me at Perth. Transforming St Johnstone was not going to be about Alex Totten. It was going to take a huge effort from everyone connected with the club.

'I knew I could confide in Bertie and use him as a sounding board. He's a genuine guy who knows the game inside out. It was important to have someone I knew and trusted by my side.'

Paton's playing career had been curtailed in his late twenties, with two serious leg breaks ending the good life which had seen him sample the cuisine of 18 continental countries. Dunfermline, during Paton's time at East End Park, were no slouches and the scalps included some fancy names from foreign fields. Italian customs' officials were among the few not to make an impression on the Paton passport. He remains the Pars' top Euro scorer.

By the time Alex Totten, a former team-mate, lured him back to football at Dumbarton, Paton was enjoying success in business, with two public houses in Fife to his name. Invited to accompany Totten to Perth, he didn't require a second time of asking.

'When a big club goes down, it can bounce back if things are sorted out. It was clear matters had been put in order off the park and I suppose Alex and I both relished the challenge. We had worked well together at Dumbarton.

'I'd been a manager in my own right but I'm happier in the assistant's role. Maybe it suits my personality better. I like to have a joke and a carry-on with the players, and a boss can't afford to get that close. Give footballers an inch and they'll take a mile, as I know from personal experience! I see my role as bridging the divide between the dressing room and the manager's office. Inevitably, I'm closer to the players than Alex. To do his job properly, he has to keep them at arms length. I've seen managers destroyed by players spotting signs of softness.

'Funnily enough, during our days as players at Dunfermline, I was the more serious one. Alex was the camp comic — on second thoughts make that read the club comic. We don't want any room for misunderstanding! Nowadays, those roles have been reversed.

'I'm no "Yes" man, and Alex wouldn't want it any other way. I'm free to speak my mind at all times. We've both been in the game a long, long time and we've developed our own ideas on how things should be done.

'Any manager has to surround himself with the right people. We feed off each other and we certainly have our share of arguments. Usually on a Friday, when he picks his team and I pick mine! We thrash it out but, in the end, he's the boss and he makes the final decision.'

Physiotherapist Jim Peacock could trace a Saints connection back to 1973, interrupted by a spell at Leicester from 1976-78. His experience was extensive, including numerous travels with the

The starting line-up.

Scotland international squad. He was happy to accept the invitation to extend his stay with the club.

'Existing staff naturally have doubts about their future when a new manager arrives,' said Peacock, whose C.V. included Perth experience under Jackie Stewart and Jim Storrie, time at Leicester with Frank McLintock, and two years with Jimmy Hill developing soccer skills in Saudi Arabia. His three-year Scotland call came from Willie Ormond after the West German World Cup sortie.

'The Saudi experience was memorable. A great deal of oil money was being invested in football and teams like Bob Paisley's Liverpool, Brian Clough's Nottingham Forest and European club sides were brought over for friendlies. The skill of the players was never in doubt. In many ways it was like Scotland 40 years ago, with youngsters kicking balls around on every street corner.

'The new board at St Johnstone were turning the club around in business terms during my first season back in the city and it was obvious when Alex Totten arrived that he knew what he wanted from the players. There was a stamp of professionalism about everything he did, starting with ordering 30 footballs so each player had one for training. Before that, we had to scramble around to get half a dozen balls.'

The board made money available during the summer and with £6,000 — a steal rather than a deal — Totten re-newed an acquaintance with striker Steve Maskrey from Queen of the South. The club invested another £7,000 in the defensive abilities of athletic defender Alan McKillop from Forfar,

Both men were prepared to sacrifice First Division status for the change in working environment, with McKillop delighted to play football on his doorstep and Maskrey contemplating bowing out of the game altogether rather than endure the final 12 months of a contract at Dumfries. East Fife tabled a bid, but Queen of the South didn't relish the prospect of Maskrey appearing in direct opposition in the campaign to come.

Totten's recruitment policy tended towards the familiar. Veteran full-back Kenny Thomson and midfield organiser Gary Thompson were among those who served him well with previous clubs. They had been over the course before and both were lured to Perth.

'Another important signing that season was Tommy Coyle. Money was tight — there had been another £5,000 for Danny Powell — and I had to sweet-talk the directors into finding another £10,000 for Tommy,' said Totten. 'That was big money for the club at the time. But I knew, like Kenny and Gary, he would be good for the team on and off the park.'

Past captain Andy Millen was in dispute with the club, but not for long. Soon, he was on his way to Alloa and full-back Don McVicar, in his second stint at Muirton, filled the vacant leadership role. Brought back to Perth from Montrose by Ian Gibson a year earlier, McVicar impressed with his work-rate and enthusiasm: 'The captaincy was an honour. I'd never been in that position before and I was delighted to take on the responsibility.'

McVicar wasn't alone in surviving the close season cull to play a crucial part in securing promotion. Among the more influential survivors were Doug Barron, a veteran from the Premier days, keeper John Balavage, Sammy Johnston and Ian Heddle.

The side was bolstered as and when money became available and, with 16 league goals to his credit, former Clyde striker Willie Watters quickly repaid a £5,000 transfer fee. The only other men to break into double figures with league goals were Coyle and Johnston. Other additions to the squad came in the form of Steve Gavin and Grant Jenkins, with players like Willie Brown, Joe McGurn and Ken Wilson leaving the scene.

It's lift-off for Totten and Saints after clinching promotion.

Coyle was to dovetail splendidly with a player his complete antithesis. If Coyle was elegance, balance, poise and subtlety, Gary Thompson, quite simply, was not. But the chunky, time-served, midfield artisan dictated the pattern of play, with an effective combination of professional wiles and no-frills tackling. Allied to Ian Heddle's unselfish, lung-bursting support play, it made for a formidable midfield unit.

Thompson, socks hugging his ankles and casting a generous shadow, looked none too athletic. But, as Totten pointed out, much the same was once said of Nobby Stiles — and he collected a World Cup medal along the way. The manager was going for a blend, and getting the ingredients spot-on.

Sammy Johnston, a 1984 youth signing, ventured an opinion echoed by many of the players to work under Alex Totten: 'He ruled the roost right from the start. When he arrived, everyone was running about daft trying to impress. It was made clear right away that he demanded 100 per cent commitment. Anything less just wasn't acceptable.

'He was a great motivator and the professionalism was unmistakable. But he knew the players had to have a laugh and a carry-on. Footballers aren't robots and there was a great spirit in the dressing room. On the mini-bus to and from Perth, Gary and Tommy were great fun. Everyone had to do their turn, whether it was singing or telling a joke. It helped bring the younger players out of their shells.'

Ironically, perhaps, given an oft-repeated commitment to entertaining and, above all, attacking soccer, it was the defensive line which contributed much to the promotion cause that season.

Keeper John Balavage, whose Saints career was threatened by a serious facial injury just weeks after signing in 1984, could boast 19 league shut-outs. The 24 goals conceded was a figure bettered in Scotland only marginally by a Celtic side cruising to the Premier title in their Centenary season.

Balavage had only four games and 14 minutes under his belt when fate dealt him an appalling blow at Hamilton. Both the upper and lower jaws were broken, along with fractures to his nose and cheekbones, when a stray boot made contact with his face. The injury toll was such that surgeons questioned the wisdom of the keeper returning to the fray.

'I don't remember much about the incident. I certainly didn't see the player coming in as I dived on the ball,' he revealed. 'My jaw was wired up for six weeks and surviving on fluids meant I shed more than a stone. That was a shock to the system, I can tell you. I didn't play again that season and the doctors were suggesting I find myself a non-contact sport. They thought I had been lucky because any higher on the head and I would almost certainly have been killed. On the other hand, you could say I was unlucky being injured at all!

'It wasn't until the following May that I got the all-clear from surgeons satisfied that the bones had knitted around the metal pins that had been inserted. In the initial stages of hospital treatment I wondered if I would play again, but by the time pre-season training under Ian Gibson came around I was keen to return.'

Consistency of selection was Totten's trump card in the promotion game, with Barron, McKillop, McVicar, Coyle and Johnston having little need to consult the team-sheet on match days. Kenny Thomson's record too was impeccable after a late August debut, Balavage missed just two starts and Ian Heddle wore the number 11 jersey on 35 occasions.

The defence was sound throughout the season. Doug Barron made his 200th club appearance, Alan McKillop fully deserved his Player of the Year awards from the supporters and John Balavage was ever reliable. With full-backs Kenny Thomson and Don McVicar automatic selections, it was far and away the meanest defensive unit in the division.

Balavage modestly maintained that McKillop and sweeper Barron bore the brunt of any attacks: 'In some matches, I rarely had to make a save. Our problem in the past had been conceding goals. We gave away 49 the previous season. Certainly those 19 shut-outs were career-best statistics for me personally but it was a tribute to all-round defensive cohesion.'

The arrival of Alex Totten heralded boss number four for 1979 signing Doug Barron, a cultured defender who had remained loyal to the club through thick and thin. He and McKillop struck up an immediate rapport to dovetail superbly at the heart of the defence.

'When I first signed for Saints, they were toiling in the First Division. Later, when we were relegated from the Premier League, no one was surprised. But most of us thought we could make a serious bid to return to the top the following season,' said Barron. 'Being relegated again meant an all-time low, but I was still enjoying my football and it never occured to me to ask away. As it turned out, escaping from the Second Division was no formality.

'It wasn't about which side played the best football. In some games, there was precious little in the way of stylish soccer and after two seasons I wondered if we'd ever pull ourselves clear. The appointment of Alex Totten, coming on top of the boardroom changes, was just the spur that was needed.'

Barron had been one of the few players to appreciate the mounting problems afflicting the club behind the scenes. Many of the personnel were oblivious to the financial traumas which had tightened the purse strings. The clear-out came as no surprise and a pre-season tournament at Rothes laid down the blueprint for success.

'The manager demanded professionalism right away. At that tournament, he teamed up players as room-mates, according to their positions in the side. For instance, I became firm friends with Alan McKillop and there's no doubt it helped foster under-standing within the team,' explained Barron.

Casting his mind back to late summertime, when invariably the living is far from easy for footballers, Totten insisted: 'At the start of the season, Bertie and I were optimistic. That pre-season tournament created harmony and team spirit in the dressing room, giving the part-time players a rare chance to get together. We got off to a great start in the league, building on a memorable 1-0 Skol Cup win against Premier League St Mirren at Paisley,' said Totten.

Not only was the opposition in a different league from Saints, in more ways than one, but just months before they had celebrated a remarkable Scottish Cup triumph, with an Ian Ferguson goal seeing off Dundee United at Hampden Park.

'They'd won the cup in May and were still on a high when we travelled to Paisley in August for the Skol Cup,' explained Ian Heddle, who struck the winning goal which brought their hosts back to earth with a bump which reverberated far beyond the immediate environs of Love Street.

'There had been no big build-up to the game, but we certainly deserved the victory. We came under considerable pressure in the last 20 minutes but that was only to be expected. St Mirren treated us as pushovers and paid the price.'

Heddle, of course, had been persuaded to commit himself to Perth by departed boss Ian Gibson and made an immediate impression on the fans by notching a debut winner at Berwick. A native of Dunfermline, he required some convincing to leave his home-town club, but with the Pars on the verge of the Premier League, he opted for guaranteed first-team football.

'Saints were a club with tradition, even if they had fallen from grace. They offered a chance for a fresh start. Ex-Dunfermline player Jim Bowie was on the staff at the time, although he was one of the players freed by Alex Totten. The change of manager actually re-inforced the Dunfermline connection, with Gary Thompson and Ken Thomson signed up. Coming from Fife, I had to put up with a lot of stick about Saints being a side of Pars rejects!'

Aberdeen, with two of their three Pittodrie goals stored for the closing 10 minutes, ended Saints Skol Cup interest. In January, the Dons — with a scrambled Robert Connor effort — ensured Saints were Scottish Cup third round casualties. But looking back

Champagne shower.

on that Muirton match, Alex Totten insisted: 'St Johnstone's performance in quagmire conditions was a credit to the Second Division. The cameras were there to record a great game and it was obvious we enjoyed the more clear-cut chances.'

Certainly, Saints shocked their more illustrious counterparts from the Granite City with the calibre of their all-action, attacking thrusts. Even Aberdeen officials confessed their 84th minute winner was cruel luck for the creative Perth players.

The manager, disappointed at the denial of a replay opportunity, nevertheless enthused over the skill, ambition and general fitness displayed by a team written off pre-match. It was yet another indication that St Johnstone were stirring from their slumbers.

In terms of sheer quality, however, that cup peformance was far from enjoying one-off status. Saints, with an unbeaten run of 14 matches stretching from the curtain raiser, joined Ally MacLeod's Ayr United in a keenly fought joust for the championship — and their encounters guaranteed pulsating entertainment.

A thrilling 3-0 triumph at Somerset Park in October was savoured by a blossoming band of travellers from the Fair City. The opening match of the season had drawn a blank, but in February Saints enjoyed a two-goal advantage at Perth. All in all, five points from six taken from their title rivals, without conceding a goal.

'Those were important results and there's no doubt the fans enjoyed the attacking play offered by both sides. Ayr hit an astonishing 95 league goals that year, with Sludden, Templeton and Walker scoring freely,' noted Totten.

The Perth defensive record prompted media interest and that was gratifying for central defender Alan McKillop: 'Being one of the few local players on the staff could have posed problems had the results been going against us. After all, Perth is a bit of a goldfish bowl. But fortunately the results were going our way and when I met supporters in the street they had only good things to say about the team.

'The run of results wasn't a surprise because it was obvious from the moment I arrived that Saints were not going to linger in the Second Division. Had I thought that, I wouldn't have stepped down a division from Forfar. At the time, it was a great move for me. As a youngster Saints had been my team and, at that point, they enjoyed a lot of success.

'It was a great season for me personally, picking up both the fans and the players' Player of the Year awards. There's so much mickey-taking in football dressing rooms that you're never too sure what the players really think of their team-mates. That award gave me particular pleasure.'

McKillop, like defensive side-kick Doug Barron, missed only one start in the entire campaign. Both players were flirting dangerously with suspension and, however peeved they might have felt, their names were absent from Totten's final team-sheet for the season.

Another match to remember unfolded on November 28, when a rampant Saints side simply dismantled Stirling Albion, managed by former Perth star John Brogan. A resounding 6-0 scoreline on the controversial artificial pitch marked the Perth club's most emphatic victory since 1969.

Midfielder Ian Heddle notched two of the goals, convinced that Saints turned on some of the best football of the season on the artificial surface at Annfield: 'We visited Stirling on the Thursday evening and trained on the park. The club had to buy special footwear with the dimpled soles for that one game. Alex Totten was encouraging us to play a passing game, the surface suited us and everyone played to form on the astroturf.'

The championship race, by now strictly a two-horse field, moved into the closing straight, with Ayr out in front by a nose.

But on April 16, short of a year after Totten took over the managerial reins at Muirton, St Johnstone clinched promotion to the First Division in style.

A Willie Watters hat-trick — his second of the season — and a goal from Sammy Johnston destroyed Arbroath in front of 2,500 Muirton fans in celebratory mood. Midfield stalwart Gary Thompson was no stranger to events of this nature. It was his fourth successive promotion party and he knew how to celebrate.

Johnston pointed out: 'We were all up in the main stand with the fans shouting and singing below us on the pitch. Gary was spraying champagne around like a Grand Prix driver and we started throwing shirts down to the crowd. The next thing they were shouting for our shorts and socks and shinguards! It was total bedlam.'

Looking back on the season, Totten said: 'We might have taken five points from Ayr United, but Ally MacLeod had the last laugh — he took the title. However, we had secured promotion, we had achieved our goal and the players quite rightly enjoyed the moment. We lost only five league games and with 59 points, ultimately just two behind the champions, we also created what I believe was a new record for St Johnstone,' said Totten.

The managerial match-day attire, incidentally, couldn't have been wetter by 5 p.m. had it been a diving suit. True to tradition, into the players' bath he went, fully clothed. That suit, like the Second Division, was a thing of the past!

Consolidation
and Cup Dreams

THE casualty count in a Premier League reduced in number from 12 to 10 comprised of Morton, Dunfermline and Falkirk. At East End Park and Brockville, they gambled on a swift return to the land of milk and honey and Old Firm gates. The personnel were retained on full-time contracts.

St Johnstone's financial situation had improved by leaps and bounds with the promotion year returning a profit of some £23,000. But no one at Muirton Park, Perth, was under any illusions — the football pay packet alone was not going to meet the mortgage.

True to their word, the directors made cash available for the manager to launch a close season sortie into the transfer market. Cowdenbeath banked £8,000 for Paul Cherry's utility talents and Stuart Sorbie was brought from Alloa for £15,000 before the warm-up programme began.

Explained Cherry, who had previously left Hearts as part of the deal which took a promising defender by the name of Craig Levein to Edinburgh: 'Everyone could see that the wheels were beginning to turn again at St Johnstone. By that time, I doubt if there was a player in the Second, or even the First Division, who didn't sit up and take notice if Saints were said to be interested.

'I was struck by the professional approach at Perth. Remember, I was coming from Cowdenbeath and a set-up where my wife was washing training kit twice a week. At Muirton, everything was freshly laundered and waiting in the dressing room before each session. Small things like that suggested the manager had experience of a big club and wanted to set similar standards in the lower division.'

On an excursion over the border, victory at Oldham was followed by three games in four days at Perth. Graham Taylor — destined to follow Bobby Robson into the England managerial post — brought his £2 million Aston Villa side north for a 2-1 win. A goal scoring display by a certain David Platt hinted that he might have some potential.

After drawing with local rivals Dundee, Leicester City were next on the agenda. Saints went down 2-1 but Alex Totten, naturally, was in optimistic mood surveying the First Division challenge. But the full-time decision at Falkirk and Dunfermline looked likely to give them the edge and, with only one place available on the up-elevator, promotion talk in Perth looked like so much wishful thinking.

The business began in earnest when Saints travelled to Edinburgh for a midweek Skol Cup date with Hearts, second to Celtic over the previous campaign. They hoped for a confidence boost but the Tynecastle side meted out capital punishment, leaving a stunned Perth boss lamenting: 'How could a team which lost only 24 goals all last season manage to lose five tonight?'

Defeat at Dunfermline followed; at Forfar, captain Don McVicar and his deputy Gary Thompson saw red and centre back Alan McKillop sustained a knee injury which threatened the curtailment of his career; even victory over Airdrie had the manager moaning: 'I'm glad I didn't pay money to watch that game.'

For McKillop, injured in an innocuous challenge with Kenny Ward, it proved the beginning of the end of his period with the Perth club. The season closed for the defender, reputedly being tracked by several clubs, after 20 minutes of the fourth match. It was more than a year before he again pulled on a blue jersey.

'I'd never been prone to injury but my studs caught in the soft ground and the knee twisted badly. I limped off but it was only weeks later, when I sought a specialist's diagnosis, that the seriousness of the injury emerged. There was damage to the ligaments, a torn cartilage and subsequently a cyst developed behind the knee. The surgeon warned that some players didn't play again after sustaining an injury like it. I underwent four separate operations and there were times over the next few months when I wondered if my career was over and done with.'

The movement of staff continued throughout the year. The fans were never quite sure if attacking midfielder Sammy Johnston was on or off the transfer list at any given moment; Billy Spence, from Raith Rovers, and Roddy Grant (£12,000 from Cowdenbeath) bolstered the frontline competition; Willie Watters went to Kilmarnock for £20,000 — while a similar sum was spent on John Irvine from East Stirling.

'When a manager buys a player he keeps his fingers crossed it's going to work out. But there are no guarantees. I've always believed competition for places is vital — there's no bigger incentive to a player than glancing over his shoulder and seeing someone willing and eager to take his place,' said Totten. 'In John's case, Celtic had been showing an interest, so we dipped in. He worked hard for me, but sadly it didn't work out.'

By November, Saints had clawed their way into third position in the championship race, but moves to strengthen the squad further were undermined by inflated transfer fees.

Saints remained on the periphery of the promotion struggle after the turn of the year but by February, any player talking of a championship coming to Perth would have been handed a strait-jacket, rather than a strip.

Before the month was out, however, there was time for a peculiar story to surface in super soaraway tabloid style. The Perth match against Kilmarnock was sponsored by the local Co-operative Funeral Services and the man-of-the-match award went to Don McVicar.

'On the Monday morning I read that I'd won myself a free funeral. I couldn't believe it! In reality, I'd won vouchers for the Co-op. But I do remember joking after the game with one of the Killie staff, so maybe that's where it came from,' said McVicar. Still, why let the truth get in the way of a ghoul of the season scoop!

On the football front, losses inflicted by Partick Thistle and Dunfermline, the ultimate champions, sounded the death knell for Saints title aspirations, leaving Alex Totten admitting: 'If we had a hill to climb before, now it's a mountain.' Fortunately, there remained the cup that cheers to bolster flagging spirits.

'Let's get this show on the road.' Graeme Souness eager for action in Doug Barron's testimonial match.

'At the start of any season you set your sights high but, looking back, consolidation in the First Division was all-important,' said the manager. 'I don't think we expected promotion right away — so a successful Scottish Cup run was always going to be welcome. For a club in our position, the money that could be generated was a prime consideration.'

For St Johnstone, the long and winding road to Hampden Park had remained something of a mystery over the two previous decades. Not since Willie Ormond mapped out the route to the 1968 semi-finals had Saints given their fans a run for their money. In this instance, the bookmakers were hardly erring on the side of generosity, quoting odds of 66-1 against blue and white ribbons adorning the silverware.

A home draw brought Stenhousemuir to Muirton in January. Ian Heddle blasted Saints into an early lead but it wasn't until the 86th minute that substitute Stuart Sorbie settled the issue. No less a figure than 'Taggart' — actor Mark McManus — conducted a television investigation into the mysteries of the Scottish Cup draw. Another home tie for Saints, Forfar or Clyde the visitors. It would hardly have tested Taggart's investigative powers to detect the smiles in Perth — here was a chance to avenge an '86 exit.

Within 10 minutes of the challenge commencing, however, Kenny Ward had wiped away the grins. But man of the match

Steve Maskrey restored home pride with a well-taken double to settle the Tayside derby. Meanwhile, the manager's post-match comments focused on speculation that Dundee had earmarked him for the vacant Dens' job.

Such a notion was quickly dispelled, with the fans assured: 'This is a great club. I'm happy here and we've a new stadium coming off. I want to be part of that.' If Alex Totten was on the move — it was with St Johnstone.

'Steve Maskrey's goal alone that day was worth the admission money. He was in superb form. In fact, a goal that year against Raith Rovers, when he collected the ball in midfield, waltzed past three defenders and finished from 20 yards remains one of the best I've ever seen.'

Next up were Morton at Greenock. The scheduled date was postponed and the teams, neck and neck in the First Division, were handed all the incentive needed for victory: a semi final tie against Rangers or Dundee United. They could now identify with a potential pools winner hanging on for confirmation of the eighth draw!

The postponement may have seen Saints into their first semi-final draw for 21 years, but still Morton remained to be negotiated. A Tommy Coyle penalty and a Roddy Grant strike counterbalanced Tommy Turner's early breakthrough, in conditions raw enough to have even an Eskimo consulting his trades union.

With Morton reduced to 10 men, Saints spurned chances and paid the price 12 minutes from time. Morton's borrowed Ibrox striker John Spencer, inevitably christened the loan-Ranger, saw John Balavage thwart his penalty kick effort. Saints were still congratulating themselves on an update of The Great Escape when Doug Robertson headed in the corner.

At Perth on March 27, Muirton Park's last Scottish Cup tie drew 8,337 fans, prompting a 20-minute delay. In the dressing room, players had been wound-up for a 7.30 p.m. kick-off. As the minutes ticked by, the tension was becoming unbearable, the nerve ends were tingling.

'The room was silent as the police let the crowd in. We could see the players were up-tight. Then, without warning, Paul Cherry

Ally's up — but Roddy Grant and Doug Barron put McCoist on the defensive in the first cup clash.

started singing — Bonnie Wee Jeannie McColl of all things! Everyone laughed, then joined in. They were relaxed when they took the field,' said Totten.

Two goals from that man Maskrey — he topped the club charts with 15 — were spliced by a Doug Robertson counter. Then local player Grant Jenkins rifled home an 81st minute shot, via the post, to trigger bedlam on the terracing.

Yet the scorer admitted: 'I made contact with the ground when I tried the shot and wondered if it would be hard enough to deflect in off the post. The next thing I knew team-mates were piling on top of me from all directions. I realised then that the ball had found the net!'

The drama continued into injury time, making a nonsense of match sponsorship from the Scottish Health Education Group. The closing minutes did as much for the heart as 40 smokes a day and fried bread for breakfast! John Balavage was forced to down John Spencer, only for John O'Neil's spot-kick to come crashing back off the bar. There was a touch of deja vu about the proceedings as Rowan Alexander was allowed space to head home a subsequent corner.

'We were hanging on by our finger nails,' confessed the manager. 'It took an eternity for the whistle to blow.' When it did, Totten bolted from the dug-out like a man possessed, scarf flailing the air. The players lapped the stadium. Then came confirmation: an Ally McCoist goal had set up a Rangers-St Johnstone Scottish Cup semi-final.

The two clubs had met on March 1, when Graeme Souness and Rangers celebrated Doug Barron's testimonial season. Alex Totten explained: 'Doug had stuck by St Johnstone through good times and bad over 10 years and deserved the best. I have the highest regard for the man both as a player and as a person. Genuine club men are few and far between nowadays. I was delighted when Graeme Sounesss brought a strong Rangers squad to Perth for the occasion.'

Barron himself admitted it was the most memorable night of his Perth career, with former Saints favourites like Alex MacDonald, John Mackay and John Brogan adding an extra element of nostalgia: 'Ally McCoist was back at Muirton in a Rangers jersey. He and I were on the Saints staff together before he left for Sunderland and we both attended Scottish under-18 trials at Largs.

'It was an emotional night for me and the only disappointment was that my father, Alex, couldn't be there. He left for Iraq on an oil contract only a matter of days before the game. My grandfather, Alex senior, was in the stand and it would have been nice had they enjoyed the occasion together.'

Perth directors Douglas McIntyre and Stewart Duff co-ordinated a variety of events designed to pay tribute to Barron. The former explained: 'I believe Doug was the first Saints player to enjoy a testimonial season since Joe Carr and Charlie McFadyen in the early sixties, and no one deserved it more. I thought if we could drum up £8,000 we would be doing well. In fact, such was the enthusiasm of the fans that we more than doubled that figure.

'At a boxing dinner in Perth, more than 200 supporters paid their own tribute to Doug. It was a great night and, I remember, one of Ian Durrant's international jerseys was auctioned to swell the fund. That was the Alex Totten connection and the manager pulled a few strings to bring Rangers to Perth for the official testimonial match.'

The chase is on for Grant Jenkins, Terry Butcher, Sammy Johnston and Richard Gough in the Cup replay.

The honours had been shared that evening. But this was the real thing. Rangers, en route to the championship, stalked the elusive treble. Saints, dismissed contemptuously by the bookies as 14-1 cannon fodder, scented glory . . . and a record payday.

The hype extended far beyond the old Perthshire boundary as the media, naturally enough, focused on Alex Totten's Ibrox history. Had the hacks had their way, the build-up to the Battle of the Blues would have been kick-started by a colourful quote from the Perth manager. All they needed was one word: revenge. Certainly, there was no lack of prompting.

'The media interest in the match was intense. Calls came in from papers and television in England. It wasn't confined to Scotland,' explained the manager. 'Everyone was on about how Rangers had sacked me and how this was my chance for revenge. I wasn't thinking in those terms — I wanted to beat Rangers because they stood between St Johnstone and their first Scottish Cup final.

'The players had never experienced anything like it in their lives. Family, friends, workmates . . . they all wanted to talk about the game, about tickets. The directors decided to retreat to Dunkeld House Hotel and, once again, that underlined the professionalism which was running through the club.'

Paul Cherry, then a supervisor with a leading insurance firm, spoke for all the players when he commented: 'It was the biggest week of our footballing lives. None of us had ever experienced media interest like it. There wasn't a day went by but there was some kind of feature in the papers. One headline talked about us as the paupers and compared our salaries, cars and houses to those of the Rangers players. I don't know where they got their information, but it was well wide of the mark. It was all a bit embarrassing but we enjoyed the limelight. In my case, breakfast television filmed a piece at the office. The ballyhoo was incredible — and the club's decision to take us to Dunkeld made perfect sense.

'We could channel our thoughts towards the game, but in a relaxed manner. It was the first time most of us had experienced this side of professional football. It gave us a taste of the good life — and we wanted more! The cup matches underlined what was possible with this club.'

Cherry, convinced high energy tablets from the health food shelves were just the thing to boost the metabolism, nearly missed out on the match of his life. He revealed: 'I was working out with the speed-ball in the Muirton gym and somehow knocked it off the frame. Obviously the tablets were working! But it hit me full in the face, cutting my nose and threatening to leave me toothless.'

Short of booking into a Trappist Monastery, there was little likelihood of a quiet countdown to the April 15 appointment at Celtic Park. So the players were encouraged to savour their spell in the spotlight. At Dunkeld the local radio station was welcomed to broadcast a phone-in for the fans.

But the man who interested the headline hunters most was quicksilver striker Steve Maskrey. Just five-years-old the last time St Johnstone survived to the semi-final phase, he faced a desperate race for fitness. A tackle at Raith, branded 'disgraceful' by Perth management, inflicted serious knee damage on Saints' number one striker.

'I knew it was a bad one whenever he connected. I was in agony and after limping to the touchline, Bertie Paton and Jim Peacock had to carry me to the dressing room,' said Maskrey. 'The next day I went to hospital for a check-up, but the knee was swollen so badly they couldn't tell the extent of the damage.

'With only 10 days before the semi-final, time wasn't on my

The Saints go marching into a semi-final replay in full cry.

side. Being off work, I was receiving physiotherapy sessions morning and afternoon. Deep down, I suppose I knew I wouldn't make it. The decision was made for me in the end, because I couldn't even kick a ball. There was no way I could have played.

'I had come to terms with the disappointment, or so I thought until the team bus approached Celtic Park. With the players singing and hammering the windows, it really was more like a supporters' bus. Then it really hit home that I was missing out on the biggest game of my career.'

Sitting with his father in the centre stand when the teams were announced, Maskrey, who had toasted cup victories over Forfar and Morton with doubles, sensed the disappointment from the Perth fans massed on the covered terracing far to his right, the traditional Rangers End. They had been hoping Saints were attempting a touch of kidology. The player, naturally, was a picture of abject dejection.

With Maskrey ruled out, and the experienced Gary Thompson suspended, the pundits assumed the Perth part-timers would retreat into a defensive shell. How else could the £73,000 side survive against an international studded Ibrox squad assembled at a cost of £6 million?

Saints had won the first psychological skirmish, winning the toss to play in blue. Rangers, the players were convinced, resented being asked to parade their change red and white strip. And with 47,374 fans filing into Parkhead, they notched up another victory in the pre-match mind games.

Explained Totten: 'I hardly slept the night before. I knew that the team was capable of doing it, but the one nagging question that kept running through my mind was: "How would they handle the pressure of the biggest game of their lives?" None of them had experienced a match, and a crowd, remotely like it. Rangers, of course, expect to be in semi-finals. They've been over the course so many times. I just wanted to see my players do themselves justice.

'The team talk at Parkhead, even if I say it myself, was probably the best I've ever given. We were in the home dressing room — Rangers were having nothing to do with that! I asked youth coach Tommy Campbell to signal when Ibrox captain Terry Butcher began to lead the players out — then every one of the Perth squad burst into song.'

'We wanted to give Rangers something to think about, to show we weren't going to go meakly like lambs to the slaughter. There was a wee Celtic steward conducting the choir as we left for the pitch! Later Terry Butcher revealed the move worked precisely as planned.

'During the match, Rangers fans were regaling the Perth support with one of those earthy songs they traditionally reserve for clubs from anywhere north of Glasgow. Then this wee man behind the dug-out chirped up: "But no' you Alex, you're a Bluenose!" Even in a game with so much at stake there was still room for a laugh.'

The tension had begun to grip after a hotel lunch spent watching the television previews. By the time the team bus, complete with police escort, swept down London Road, Saints were in full cry. Bemused Rangers supporters soaking up the atmosphere in tandem with an alfresco aperitif were treated to a full-blooded choral arrangement of Bonnie Wee Jeannie McColl!

But to the match itself: direct from the kick-off, Saints tore into the pre-match script, and left it shredded. A bold attacking strategy caught Rangers off guard. Grant Jenkins, operating in central midfield, snuffed out influental playmaker Ray Wilkins;

Paul Cherry and Doug Barron clamped down on strike duo Ally McCoist and Kevin Drinkell; while Wyatt Earp himself couldn't have matched the marshalling job Kenny Thomson did on touchline star Mark Walters!

Up front, gung-ho Roddy Grant rattled England stalwart Terry Butcher and million-pound-plus Scotland partner Richard Gough; skipper Don McVicar was inspired; and keeper Balavage was rarely troubled. But it was a heroic 13-man performance which defied Rangers and, ultimately, deserved greater reward than the scoreless draw and a replay cash jackpot.

Paul Cherry collected the Mr Superfit man of the match accolade for an immaculate performance against McCoist. He acknowledged: 'Obviously that's an award to cherish and to show the grandchildren one day. But while individual awards are nice to receive, the most important thing is the team performance. That day we were superb.

'It was vital not to lose an early goal and as the game progressed I thought we created the better chances. By half-time, with the match nicely poised, we did begin to think the final was in reach. They really only had one chance when McCoist was through in the closing minutes. Players aren't supposed to think about money during a match, but I thought the bonus was about to be snatched away! Luckily, Ally didn't find the net. Soon after, the final whistle sounded and we had exceeded everyone's wildest expectations.'

The manager insisted: 'Every one of my players brought credit to themselves, the club and the First Division. They were magnificent. Rangers weren't allowed to play. It was a brilliant, professional performance that they can all recollect with pride.'

At no stage did Rangers produce the form which secured the Premier title in later weeks. But super Saints were immense on one of the most marvellous afternoons the club has ever known.

They laid on a special train at Perth Station, for the first time in years, and more than 60 buses headed west. The scene as the exhausted Saints took their bow before a delirious blue and white bedecked segment of Parkhead terracing will live long in the memory.

While Perth fans danced in the sunshine, Rangers manager Graeme Souness (who had earlier defied a touchline ban to cajole his team) faced the Press. His comments were brief, and to the point: 'I would like to think we can play better than that. I'm just glad to get a second chance. Thank you gentlemen.'

Sadly, this historic day for St Johnstone and their supporters was tinged with deep sorrow. As the fans headed home on an emotional high, radios brought confirmation of the rising death toll at Hillsborough. The dark shadow cast that day from Sheffield was to stretch a long, long way.

The Tuesday replay saw Saints' resources, with an injured Tommy Coyle ruled out of contention, stretched to the limit. Maskrey, short of full fitness, was introduced to the starting line-up after an overnight camp at Dunblane Hydro.

Said Maskrey: 'On the Saturday I had been delighted for the boys, but not having played I felt a bit removed from the celebrations in the dressing room. Obviously I wished I'd been out on the park. I was far from being fully fit but I was pleased to get a chance in the replay.

'The knee had improved since the weekend but I still had trouble kicking. It's a pity it was my right leg rather than the one for standing on that had been damaged! In the first 20 minutes I took a bit of a tumble and that didn't help matters.'

After the weekend high, the Perth management team faced mission impossible and they knew it. Totten explained: 'The part-time players had given their all on the Saturday. Calling on them to scale the heights twice within four days was asking too much. Bertie, who actually scored a replay goal for Dunfermline to help beat Saints in that 1968 semi-final, tried to help me lift them. But they never found the missing sharpness and elementary mistakes cost us the game.'

Rangers, back in their beloved blue before a crowd again in excess of 40,000, secured a 14th minute advantage through Mark Walters and, well into injury time at the interval, Gary Stevens hammered another nail into the Perth coffin. Rangers, doubtless encouraged by weekend words of wisdom from the Ibrox management, turned on the screw and no little style.

Within seconds of the re-start, Saints were playing only for their professional pride as the defence was caught cold by Kevin Drinkell. Finally, prolific Scotland striker Ally McCoist pounced, taking full advantage of weary limbs to round-off the scoreline at

Players and fans form a mutual admiration society.

4-0. Saints' impossible dream had faded away in Glasgow's cool night air.

Even Mr Superfit, Paul Cherry, winner of six supporters club awards that season, admitted to exhaustion: 'Straight from the kick-off that night you could sense Rangers were hungrier and more determined than they had been on the Saturday. Some of our players had been working as normal on the Monday and others were carrying knocks. We had run ourselves into the ground in the first match and the replay came too soon for part-time legs and lungs. But the semi-final was an important springboard for everything that followed.'

Totten admitted: 'Rangers won and they deserved to win. But that semi-final brought St Johnstone back into the picture. The players involved in both ties massively enhanced the club's reputation and their efforts secured a £97,000 pay-out which could be invested for the future.'

Saints' season to all intents and purposes, ended at Parkhead. The players admitted that the return to normality was hard to bear. Mentally, many of them were focusing on little more than the summer holidays. But there remained five league chores to complete before looking out the tanning lotion.

The Cup cash didn't linger in a bank account, accruing interest. Immediately after overcoming Morton, the board approved

£30,000 expenditure to obtain the signature of competitive Clydebank captain Mark Treanor, while defender David Martin was brought from Queen of the South for £4,000. Already, the demands of a new season were being anticipated.

Before the end of the season, Saints announced a shirt sponsorship deal with Dundee-based textiles, plastics and packaging group Low and Bonar. The company laid their durable floorcoverings at Saints' new home and produced the artificial playing surface on the adjacent all-weather pitch. The deal was hailed as the best in the First Division and in return the strip, by now manufactured by Bukta, would carry the 'Bonar' logo.

Director Allan Campbell explained: 'The chairman was asked to phone Roland Jarvies of Low and Bonar in Dundee. He explained he had been attending Muirton with his sons and wondered if he could help the club. For a company with an international outlook, match sponsorship wasn't much use to them but after seeing the plans for the new stadium, club and company agreed a unique sponsorship deal.'

On the pitch, Saints collected a meagre single point from a possible 10 as March merged with April. At last, the curtain came down with a 2-0 defeat at Clyde, memorable only for an injury-time penalty which threw the toiling Glasgow club a vital First Division lifeline — and a managerial rage.

'I was furious. After all that had gone before, the players let themselves down at Firhill that day. Of course it was an anti-climax and of course Clyde were battling for survival — but that didn't excuse our attitude. It was unprofessional and I simply wasn't prepared to tolerate that kind of performance. The players were given something to think about over the summer.'

It may have been the end of another season for the employees. But it signalled the end of an era for the Perth club. Muirton Park, home since 1924, was about to be erased from the city landscape. Two weeks earlier, there had been 6,728 present to say goodbye on April 29, 1989.

Ayr United's John Sludden, a former Perth player, secured a place in Scottish fotball trivia as the last striker to trouble the Muirton rigging. But it was a day for unabashed nostalgia, for strolls down memory lane and for quiet reflection.

The club welcomed in the fans for a morning of mourning.

The strain game: Peacock, Totten and Paton feel the pressure.

Then the wake began in earnest. The Perth and District Pipe Band played while fans sought out commemorative envelopes, souvenir programmes and lapel badges. Taking the final whistle as their cue, they swarmed over the barricades.

It wasn't quite Wembley re-visited, but many a lawn, the manager's included, was to boast a section of the hallowed turf. Perth fanzine 'Wendy Who?' (as in Wendy Saints Go Marching In!) had the decency to furnish their readership with a complimentary plastic fork to further their horticultural endeavours! Out trooped the players, in various stages of undress, to mingle with the fans and distribute memorabilia, and the tannoy blasted out 'The Saints' for Auld Lang Syne.

Still there was time for tradition — the inevitable announcement to re-unite father and son — until finally a spirited rendition of the side's unofficial, adopted anthem 'Bonnie Wee Jeannie McColl' assailed the ears of the lingering few. It was time to go home.

Shaggy-haired striker Grant Jenkins, perhaps more than any of the players, knew what the occasion meant to the older fans. 'As a youngster I used to get the bus in from Dunning every other week to see Saints. John Connolly was my great hero in those days. Footballers tend to be a sentimental lot. Probably because the memories have to last a long time. I certainly found myself taking a stroll around the ground that evening, just like many of the supporters.'

Under the stand, Alex Totten and Geoff Brown found themselves sharing a bath with ex-Ranger Derek Johnstone, on duty for the BBC; former club chairman Alex Lamond admitted he had donned 'the funeral suit' for the occasion; and, with darkness closing in, the wood panelled Muirton boardroom was awash with memories, and not a few farewell libations.

For Muirton, Read McDiarmid

DAYS after the announcement that Geoff Brown and his colleagues had accepted the most daunting of business challenges, the rumour factory moved into full scale production. Within months, it was whispered, Muirton Park would be razed to the ground and the city could prepare for the opening of another showhouse.

The cynics were wide of the mark on both counts. In fact, Muirton Park survived until the summer of 1989 to be replaced, not by homes, but by a superstore. Far from signalling the demise of Perth's professional football interests, the multi-million-pound property deal secured the future of St Johnstone and propelled the club into an unprecedented spell in the national limelight.

A family atmosphere was fostered deliberately and for the first time in many years local parks and playing fields witnessed youngsters parading St Johnstone colours in abundance. Sports shops reported that demand even for the Scotland garb was outstripped by the clamour for local colours as Saints swept upwards and onwards.

On July 14, 1989, St Johnstone officially took possession of the country's first custom-built, all-seater football stadium which, in only 10 months, took shape on former agricultural land on the western periphery of the city. On August 19, the serious business began at McDiarmid Park, with 7,267 patrons easing through the computerised turnstiles for a First Division league fixture with Clydebank.

The standards of safety and comfort were praised universally at the first top grade football stadium to be built in Britain for decades and the opening of the £5.5 million showpiece development provided a blueprint for clubs coming to terms with the verdicts of post mortems conducted in the wake of tragedies at Bradford's Valley Parade and Sheffield's Hillsborough.

There were uninterrupted views of an international class playing surface for 10,169 paying customers — later boosted to 10,721 — from individual, rainbow coloured seats nestling in four covered stands. Officials from football clubs, small and mighty, made tracks to Perth to admire, to envy and to learn. Was this the way to 21st Century sporting facilities?

Yet three years earlier, St Johnstone Football Club were rarely registering on the pools' coupons, far less the national consciousness. Muirton Park, home since 1924, was wasting away. A capacity once nudging 30,000 had been slashed to 5,000 and safety fears for the designated sports ground prompted Tayside Regional Council to caution that no more than 2,500 spectators would be allowed access without the implementation of essential remedial work.

St Johnstone, in common with other clubs north of the border, had been ordered to meet certain safety criteria by the Scottish Secretary prior to embarking on a brief foray into the Premier League during 1983-84. The following year, flames engulfed the traditional wooden structure of Bradford's Valley Parade, claiming the lives of 52 victims, with a further 200 suffering extensive injuries.

In the autumn of 1985, the club applied for a safety certificate from Tayside Region, two months after an inspection team scrutinised the decrepit grandstand and crumbling, open terracing. Words, rather than money, had been spent . . . buying little more than time. An estimated £1 million was needed to transform the Dunkeld Road relic.

Geoff Brown recalled the club's predicament: 'The playing surface at Muirton Park was in fine condition. Unfortunately, nothing else could match it. Little had been done to the ground since the club featured in the Premier League, and it showed.

'Terracing exposed to the elements needs on-going attention during the close season. But the club didn't have the money for repairs and, to be fair, the crowds were hardly putting the facilities under pressure. Had attendances been bigger, the state of the

Muirton Park . . . pensioned off.

barriers might have endangered lives. The concrete had been eaten away and they were being held up by wooden supports.'

Workmen assigned from G.S. Brown Construction carried out a basic patch-up project. Around £10,000 was spent levelling concrete slabs and the like. Tayside Region relented and eased their crowd cap to 5,000. By the turn of the year, the capacity had been boosted to 10,000.

'We drew Aberdeen at Perth in the third round of the Scottish Cup and that certainly put the cat amongst the pigeons. We spent around £3,500 creating a segregation barrier, dividing the ground for home and visiting supporters. As it turned out, Aberdeen who had contributed generously towards the bill, returned 2,600 tickets and the money went down the drain.'

Brown highlighted the part played by the Perthshire business community in hauling the club back onto its feet. Revenue from advertising hoardings and programme sales leapt from £2,000 to £16,000 within 12 months, giving a financial and cosmetic boost to dilapidated Muirton Park. Sponsorship moved ahead from £2,400 in 1986 to £38,000 for season '87-88 and continued to spiral upwards.

Allan Campbell, too, paid tribute to the response from the commercial sector, as the board tapped a sympathetic vein: 'The priority was to establish a sound business base for the club and the directors bombarded contacts for backing. Football clubs are treated differently from other lines of business. There was a desparation in the area to see the club turned around, so it wasn't such a hard sell as it might have been. There was enormous goodwill and that helped turn the financial tide.'

The directors placed the entire club structure under the microscope. Monitoring the main entrance on match day revealed that one in six of the crowd strolled through the front door without paying their way; match sponsorship was sought actively; businesses parted with £250 for advertisement boards, the deal including season tickets; and Saints went on to toast shirt sponsorship in the form of 'The Famous Grouse' whisky.

'It was the first shirt deal in the club's history and the sponsors saw it as a community gesture, rather than as a commercial venture. At first the company was wary of the brand name on replica strips, fearing accusations of flaunting alcohol in the faces of children,' said Brown. 'But we sealed a two-year deal and the £6,000 was a marvellous boost to club finances.'

Campbell noted: 'The club's predicament turned out to be even more severe than we'd suspected at the outset. Everyone involved accepted it was going to be a challenge, but I don't think we really anticipated the scale of the problem and the time it would consume.'

Curiously, the first match sponsorship package was sold in a city centre bar, to an Englishman! A guest of local lawyers with the oval, rather than the round ball prompting the trip north, he succumbed to the sales pitch. Later, he introduced another sponsor from the other side of Hadrian's architectural legacy.

A deal was struck with Matchwinner, to supply kit to the club worth £5,000 — that had happened only once before — and after taking the aid shop losses on the chin, a £40,000 annual loss was turned into £4,500 rental profit.

The rickety state of the tinderbox grandstand, however, posed problems quickly slotted into the insurmountable file. A mere third of the bench seating was open to the public, and then only because fire prevention measures had been introduced as part of the licensed social club at ground level. The north section and centre stand, directors' box included, were ruled out of bounds on safety grounds, post-Bradford.

'We tackled some of the safety work to re-open the centre section and directors' box, bringing the capacity up to 940. The north stand remained taboo. The Bradford disaster highlighted

The final whistle for Muirton Park.

the dangers apparent at ageing football grounds the length and breadth of the country and, to be honest, Muirton was a potential death-trap, especially when fans were allowed to smoke. It would have been financially impossible to modernise the stand as it stood. That was never really a viable option.

'We were toying with the idea of creating a new stand at the town end of the ground, where there was enough land to create a development encompassing hospitality facilities and office accommodation for rent. That might have been the way ahead, but for the superstore deal.

'Muirton Park was far from exceptional. No way was it unique. A look around the country today pinpoints any number of football stadiums in the same predicament. Clubs have to address the problems sooner or later and St Johnstone may have opened their eyes to possibilities.

'Prior to Saints making the decision to move from their traditional setting, I'm sure there had been any number of football clubs approached with similar deals. In fact, across the UK, around 10-20 projects were probably mooted but knocked back by clubs hide-bound by tradition. Directors seemed to think it would be like moving a graveyard. They shied away from the whole idea before thinking through the possibilities.

'The fact is that no one had seriously considered moving their ground before St Johnstone took the initiative. Boards feared upsetting their supporters and shifting the ground was considered taboo. Another factor was that the Football Ground Improvement Trust rules allowed for say 25 per cent grants towards upgrading existing facilities — but they didn't want to know about financial input to a new stadium. Unfortunately, it took the Hillsborough tragedy to change attitudes.'

Brown pointed out that football grounds created in the Victorian era or after the turn of the century invariably sprang up on the periphery of city or town. Long ago, they were corralled by housing and commercial developments and swallowed up by spreading suburbs or central shopping zones.

'The prospect of moving from the Dunkeld Road site didn't deter us from pursuing the options open to us. Football grounds are used only on rare occasions and it makes sense to remove them from the heart of built-up areas, freeing the land for uses likely to generate more capital.'

The chairman noted that St Johnstone's homes, at the Recreation Ground and Muirton Park itself, both emerged from land on the edge of town. Why should it have been deemed radical to contemplate building on a greenfield, boundary site in the late 1980s?

'When the new directors first became involved in the club, the main priority was to see football surviving. That was the goal first and foremost in our minds. St Johnstone was to be a hobby for us, and that's still the way it is. But no one really appreciated how much time and effort would be devoted to the club.'

With Brown's fortunes generated over twenty years on building sites around Scotland, here was ready-made material for cynics questioning his reasons for moving into a new ball game. He recalled: 'I was well aware of the stories circulating in the area. They were saying Muirton would be turned into houses and flats. But if I'd been looking to buy land I can think of an awful lot more suitable acreage.

'I reckon, after clearance costs, the six and a half acres were worth only £125,000. The rumour mongers seemed oblivious to

Progress report in January, 1989.

the fact that G.S. Brown Construction had never been involved in city flat developments, preferring greenfield sites for residential housing. Had I been looking for land I'd have looked elsewhere, I can assure you.

'I suppose some of the sniping did get through to us. As a paid managing director it would have gone with the territory, but everyone involved behind the scenes was putting in immense amounts of time and effort voluntarily. They simply wanted to see St Johnstone prosper on and off the field of play.'

The first inkling that this provincial Perth club was to prove a pacesetter for the rest of the country came, via the telephone, in December, 1986. Jim Glass of the Glassedin development company, later involved with Hearts at the Millerhill relocation project in Edinburgh, contacted Brown at his Carse of Gowrie home. Would St Johnstone be interested in moving to a 10,000 capacity, all-seated stadium?

'I remember my immediate reaction was: what will the cynics make of this one? There was an annual meeting of shareholders coming up on a Sunday before Christmas and, after our earlier rights issue, it was sure to see the biggest turn-out in the club's history. That was the time and place to put the suggestion — it was no more than that — to those immediately involved with the club. It came up under any other competent business, and it came as a bombshell, even to my fellow directors.

'I hadn't uttered a single word on the idea to the directors, simply because I wanted everyone present to consider the project dispassionately and make whatever decisions were necessary. I put it to the shareholders that if they agreed to the idea in principle, the club itself could pursue planning permission for the site.

'I'd made it clear there was no question of accepting anything less than a 10,000 all-seated and all-covered stadium. There were one or two mumbles from the floor but the motion was passed well-nigh unanimously. Those present could see that the move was on par with a family leaving behind a fraying tent to take up residence in a smart, luxury apartment. It was an historic decision for the club.'

Meddle with football and emotional minefields open up in all directions. The Muirton postbag included 50 letters furiously protesting against the removal of the standing option. Others argued the case for a stadium catering for 20,000 spectators.

But the Perth board of directors had done their homework. Perth and her hinterland, with a population of little more than 125,000, enjoyed a strictly limited catchment area for the football club. With remarkable vision, the club demanded an all-seated stadium. Later the government and the international authorities pursued similar goals. But any stadium stretching beyond the 10,000 capacity would have crippled the club once again financially.

Brown's stance was, and remains, straightforward. The new stadium would be built for St Johnstone fans. Opposition supporters would find themselves persona non grata if Perth fans were ever to respond in sufficient numbers to occupy the seats available. That is still the case.

It's not a popular viewpoint to express in football circles. Scottish soccer, after all, has milked the Old Firm travelling fraternity for many a moon. More than a few clubs require the seasonal visits from Rangers and Celtic to keep the frown from the bank manager's countenance.

But Brown explained: 'If the fans of teams like Rangers, Celtic

Home sweet home: McDiarmid Park.

and Hearts can't get tickets for matches at Perth because they've all gone to Saints fans I would be delighted. That's what the stadium was built for. It would be marvellous to see the club generating sufficient fans to fill the ground.

'There's no obligation on any club to make tickets available for visiting fans, apart from Scottish Cup ties when there's an onus to offer a percentage of seating not already acquired by season ticket holders. Why should a side like St Johnstone to all intents and purposes throw away home advantage against the Old Firm by letting their fans be the majority? That's always been a major factor in the success of the two big Glasgow sides.'

In focusing attention on a 10,000 capacity stadium, the directors of St Johnstone pointed to the previous excursion in the Premier League when gates averaged out at 4,000. The logic was simple: why should St Johnstone pick up the financial millstone accompanying more extensive seating plans, with guaranteed sell-outs only when the Old Firm come to town?

'What's the point in presenting the likes of Rangers and Celtic with the advantage straight from the kick-off? You might as well play every game in Glasgow.'

Looking down the Carse of Gowrie, the chairman instanced Dundee United. Despite consistent league performances over nearly 20 years, crowned with the Premier championship and valiant cup campaigns at home and abroad, Tannadice crowd figures averaged out around 8,000, when Old Firm gates were left out of the calculations.

'During our promotion winning season, we lured back much of the latent support and gates averaged 5,750. They increased in the Premier arena, where the club budgeted for an average of 7,000. How many clubs can, in effect, say they're averaging gates of nearly seven per cent of their total catchment area?

'Times have changed since the days when football attracted mass audiences. There are so many alternative forms of entertainment competing with the sport nowadays. Once, football was the cloth-cap game for working men finishing the shift, going to the pub and on to the match. Those days disappeared long ago. Even shopping is an option late into a Saturday evening now.'

That very factor worked in St Johnstone's favour when pushing on with planing permission to make Muirton Park a marketable commodity. With several superstore concerns rumoured to be angling for a Perth presence during the tail-end of the eighties consumer boom, the Dunkeld Road site, in tandem with the neighbouring Perth Ice Rink, faced serious competition.

Six other sites were in the running for superstore planning permission, but there would be only one winner, in accordance with Tayside Region's Structure Plan for commercial development in the Fair City. Saints' were marked down as losers in some quarters, after Perth and Kinross District Council red-carded the proposals. But the ball was bounced into the region's arena for the final decision.

Initial joint moves with Perth Ice Rink foundered and the neighbours went their own way to secure new homes. The latter enjoyed grant aid and Gannochy Trust in-put towards the splendid Dewar's Rinks facilities developed at Glover Street. For St Johnstone, it was very much a d-i-y operation.

'We received planning permission for Muirton Park in March 1987. There were several major obstacles to be overcome en route, including a Section 50 agreement with Tayside Region. In layman's terms that ensured no superstore could be developed until the new football ground was ready for the club,' said Brown.

It's all smiles for Geoff Brown and Bruce McDiarmid on opening day.

The attitude of Perth and Kinross District Council irked the Perth board of directors. Believing they were trying to achieve something for the city, not just the football club, they anticipated more enthusiastic support from the City Chambers. Instead, it remained lukewarm at best. Councillors seemed intent on fending off the intrusion of another superstore on the Muirton site. They favoured land further removed from the central area.

'It wasn't a deliberate case of stopping the St Johnstone plans. Rather, the majority of councillors simply didn't want another superstore. But the reality was always going to be that one would get the go-ahead from Tayside Region. As it transpired, we enjoyed unamimous support from the regional representatives. They seemed to appreciate how the broader community could benefit.'

Another factor warranting serious consideration was the fate of the popular Muirton Park Social Club, which would disappear with the ground — taking with it £45,000 from the club's annual accounts. Director Douglas McIntyre, whose experience in the licensed trade helped maximise potential profits through social clubs in Perth and Crieff, was well aware of the sensitivity of the subject.

'The social club income was crucial to the football business. Under the previous regime, money from the one-armed bandit had been the lifeblood of St Johnstone. Without it, the bank might have pulled the plug,' he acknowledged. 'Members feared we might leave them in the lurch. The problem was locating the right sort of premises and that took longer than anticipated. The deal for the former Tay Motel ran into land ownership technicalities, again holding up progress, and no one was more delighted than the board when the new club opened in the spring of 1991.

'We always felt Muirton, with a 10,000 catchment area and few licensed premises, was the best place for the social club. We didn't want to tamper with a winning formula and the protracted negotiations were frustrating. But we were delighted for the fans when the deal finally gelled.'

Initial estimates for a seated stadium, without cover, hovered around £1.4 million. That was dismissed as a non-starter by Saints, with the board determined to dig in all the way down the line. They had spelled out their shopping list in determined fashion right from day one.

Brown explained: 'There were some hard decisions to make at the time. Insisting on our initial demands meant we might have a new stadium, but there would be no cash left over. Had we settled for some covered terracing or uncovered seating there would have been money to play with — something like £400,000, in fact.

'Clearly that was a serious temptation. It would have secured finance for strengthening the team. But we knew it would be difficult and expensive to add on stands within the bowl-shaped area at a future date if cash did become available. We opted for a win or bust strategy, believing it to be in the best interests of the club and the city.'

Brown and his fellow director McIntyre, in particular, found their lives dominated by the stadium/superstore package literally day after day through 1987 and the spring of the following year. Brinkmanship and the inevitable stress which went with it, was the order of the day after superstore giants Asda Stores PLC moved into the frame.

Another in a growing list of offers from the company came forward in June, 1988. The would-be buyers wanted personal

The Man in Manchester United: Sir Matt Busby.

guarantees and indemnities from St Johnstone and the individual directors, assuring that the club would be playing in a new home within a given time-span, clearing the way for Asda at Muirton Park. Failure would have left club and board members facing hefty financial penalties.

Brown said: 'They were told in no uncertain terms that this was a non-starter. If they wanted it so badly, they could go ahead and build the stadium themselves — provided it met our full requirements. For two weeks we heard nothing, so I sent a fax to say that we wanted an answer within 24 hours or the deal was off. They came back within the hour to say it was still under consideration. Their figures were being fed into a computer to see if they added up.'

The following day, back came the news: the deal wasn't dead, but it looked like pegging out. The countless man hours committed to the project seemed certain to count for naught. A mood of depression hung over Muirton Park.

But at 4.30 p.m. on a June afternoon, the call came through from Asda: the price was right. If the company could save on the projected £4 million then being offered to Saints, by building the stadium themselves, there would be no argument from the club.

Brown explained: 'I had no hesitation in agreeing to that. I knew there was no way the stadium could be built for even £4 million, given inflation in the building world. The company felt the price was over the top — later we heard that the deal came within £20,000 of not going ahead — but they were willing to press on. We were elated.

'We attracted flak at the time, and later, for not including a sprinkler system and undersoil heating during the development phase. But the simple fact was that the money wasn't available. Even a sprinkler would have cost £15,000. We might have cut back on quality seating — but we wanted the best for the fans. It was all a question of priorities and undersoil heating, costing more than £100,000, simply wasn't feasible.

'The district council had given the stadium plans their unanimous backing in March. But it wasn't until October 1 that I was in a position to tell 1,961 fans attending the Partick Thistle match that the contracts had been signed. The announcement was made over the tannoy at the interval.'

Remarkably, 174 individual plans had been prepared painstakingly for the projected football ground. Saints certainly weren't slow to furnish Asda with detailed plans for the dream home and, on September 30, building contractors Miller Construction received the 'go-ahead' to start work come Monday morning at Newton of Huntingtower farmland hugging the Crieff Road.

The task was enormous. The valley-shaped site had to be levelled before construction could begin in earnest. That meant the removal of 24,000 cubic metres of topsoil and a further 88,000 cubic metres dug out of the terrain. Quite a feat of landscape gardening! The workforce on-site peaked at 140.

The 17-acre package of land secured through the generosity of Perthshire farmer Bruce McDiarmid was a crucial element in the tortuous wheeling and dealing which had consumed so much of the board's attention month after month.

Initial links were forged between club and landowner through Bob Reid, a local quantity surveyor and nephew of Bruce McDiarmid. St Johnstone owned Muirton Park and the adjacent Florence Place car park and they had taken some time to clear the path to the new stadium with feu superior Lord Mansfield, whose

The all-star cast on opening night.

family had gifted the Dunkeld Road land. Any new stadium, however, would have remained little more than a pipedream but for the McDiarmid connection. In an intricate and, at times, exasperating jigsaw, this was the telling piece.

'The going rate for the land would have been around £400,000 and quite simply, St Johnstone simply couldn't look at that kind of money. We couldn't even raise a quarter of that sum. But we hoped Bruce McDiarmid might be interested in helping out the club, and the city of Perth,' said Brown.

'The land was made available to Saints because Bruce saw the club as being an important part of Perth life. He saw this as a gift to the people of the city and I would like to think Bruce saw how hard people had worked voluntarily in the interests of the football club.'

The berry and barley fields were transformed, as the bachelor farmer, in his late seventies, accepted a 20 per cent shareholding in St Johnstone and, at the board's insistence, the honorary presidency of the football club.

'I'd been a Saints supporter since my schooldays although, like so many others, I'd lost interest in the club. But the chairman and the directors were forward-thinking and I felt their ambitions would be to the benefit of Perth as a whole, not just the football team. It was a project which began with a vague idea and took shape gradually. There was no grandiose scheme being hatched,' said McDiarmid.

'The ground, and the team's success, has been good for the area. The creation of such a beautiful stadium was enough to generate support and interest from people who had given up on the game. It has attracted an enormous amount of publicity, bringing the city to national prominence, and the spin-off benefits have been enjoyed by us all. I was honoured to have the new ground in my name and I hope the club enjoys further success in the years ahead.'

The name of the ground was approved without dissent at the annual meeting of the club shareholders in December, 1988. They, like the directors, were fully aware of the immense impact Bruce McDiarmid's decision would have on the sporting life in Perth for decades to come.

Several fans lobbied for the stadium to reflect the contribution of former manager Willie Ormond to the club's history but Brown was adamant: 'Let no one underestimate what Bruce McDiarmid has done. Without his generosity, there would have been no ground for St Johnstone.' But the supporters' suggestion that part of the ground be named in honour of the late Saints and Scotland manager found ready favour in the boardroom.

Later, the chairman was to emphasise: 'Willie Ormond stands out like a beacon in St Johnstone's history. We are well aware of his immense contribution to this football club.'

With Muirton Park scheduled to bow out of Scottish football on April 29, 1989, work continued apace on the structure emerging little more than a mile away on the Crieff Road. In the early stages, Saints had toyed with the idea of re-scheduling early matches in the 1989-90 season away from home. There was also talk of playing, even if the stadium remained half finished. As it transpired, the project went like the proverbial dream.

Inevitably, the building work attracted further media attention, in the wake of the dreadful events which unfolded at Sheffield on the day Saints savoured their Scottish Cup semi-final at Celtic Park.

Later, Geoff Brown was to welcome Lord Justice Taylor to McDiarmid Park, before the publication of the influential Hillsborough Report. The eminent visitor expressed himself delighted with the many safety factors built-in to the newest stadium in the country, as he surveyed the Perth facilities.

He toured the nerve centre of the McDiarmid operation — the 3000-seater West Stand, incorporating everything from dressing rooms, gym and managerial office at pitch level to boardroom, restaurant and hospitality suites above. The club had liaised closely with the emergency services throughout the development phase, aiming to make McDiarmid the safest sports ground in the land.

Computer technology was utilised at the turnstiles, complementing closed circuit television monitors; broad exits from the stands were installed at regular intervals, allowing spectators emergency access to an extensive running track fringing the international standard playing surface, measuring 115 x 75 yards.

Every spectator enjoyed an individual tip-up seat and an uninterrupted view of the pitch. In the West Stand, fans luxuriated in legroom unrivalled at any sports ground in Britain while club members enjoyed the comfort of padded seating. Safety, style and comfort were the watchwords.

The sprawling car park could cater for 1,000 vehicles and a further 100-plus supporters' buses and, alongside the stadium, an all-weather sports pitch was created. The £350,000 bill was shared between club, district council and the Football Trust. The football team could utilise the facility for training purposes and, at other times, the community could make full use of the complex, complete with separate dressing room accommodation.

Little was reminiscent of Muirton Park. The floodlights, however, had been salvaged. Acquired through a combination of Football Trust grant aid and a wedge of the transfer cash accrued when Ally McCoist went on to further his soccer studies with Sunderland, they required little more than a galvanising coat and new bulbs.

Said Brown: 'We were in unknown territory for a football club, but we were determined the stadium should put Perth on the map. We wanted to create something the community would be proud of — and I think we succeeded. It's now part of the local tourist trail and we've had parties from clubs too numerous to count looking at the facilities. On one occasion, there was a coach party including representatives of every non-league club in England.

'Hillsborough was uppermost in our minds from the safety aspect. We were left pretty much to get on with it by other clubs and neither the Scottish Football Association or the Scottish

League stood in our way. Initially, many clubs seemed dubious about what we were doing — but the move had a major impact on football throughout the country. Without McDiarmid Park would there have been talk about building a new national stadium away from Hampden, for instance?'

Eyebrows were raised when touring parties discovered that the ubiquitous executive box was seen to be posted missing. Brown admits it was down to personal preference, or rather, distaste for that particular brand of corporate entertainment.

'Long before I became directly involved in football, I had attended glamour matches as a guest of companies with access to these facilities. But I've always believed an important element in football is being caught up in the atmosphere of a game, and I found sitting behind glass frontages frustrating. It was like watching television with the sound turned down. It wasn't my idea of football.

'At Tannadice, I'd seen the matches with Barcelona, with Manchester United and with Gothenburg. These were momentous events in the club's history but in the executive box I felt cut off from the game. Another factor we took into consideration was that many local businessmen had made friendships through the club and enjoyed each other's company in the stand.'

The alternative explored was a number of hospitality suites providing a range of meals, snacks and refreshment options, complemented by the comfort on offer in the West Stand. In addition to bringing money into the club every season, the facilities could be utilised throughout the year for all manner of events. The same could not be said of executive boxes, used only on Saturday afternoons and the occasional midweek evening.

'In the past, football was run simply as a game, rather than a business. I remember one director telling me that an awful lot of money passed through his hands, but none of it seemed to stick. The business acumen simply wasn't there. The money was allowed to filter away, instead of being ploughed into stadium modernisation or cash-generating areas of investment.

'There was plenty of talk about Yuppie football from the so-called traditionalists. Fair enough, it can be a hefty sum to pay to watch a football match but if people believe they're getting value for money what's the problem? On the eve of the Premier

The exchange of pennants.

campaign St Johnstone had sold nearly 3,000 season tickets. That was by far a record for the club and it brought in around £300,000. But the 200 people who opted for our Premier, Executive and Hospitality memberships injected around £200,000.

'At the same time, fans can enjoy their football at a reasonable price elsewhere in the stadium, knowing that the money raised is being spent on improving the quality of player they're seeing in the team. They can see the result of the club's business strategy on the park.

'In gaining promotion from the Second Division, the club spent around £50,000 — more money than any of our rivals — but still returned a £23,000 profit. The manager's squad was strengthened during our two years in the First Division and the move into the Premier League heralded investment on an unprecedented scale for this club. That's an indication of our ambition, but money must be generated to compete at the top level. The directors will not spend money the club cannot afford.

'The businessman is a vital element in improving the prospects of success for the club — and every fan can share in that success, no matter how healthy their bank balance. Many professionals have offered their time and expertise without charge, whether it's in the field of accountancy, surveying, architecture or engineering, simply because they want to contribute to the club they support.'

Ever aware of the club's merchandising potential, the range of souvenirs mushroomed; the match programme, edited by Paul Smith, was to be rated among the best in the Premier League; McDiarmid Park snackbars, offering live video screen coverage of the football action, carried a variety of branded food and drink; connoisseurs of the grape could grapple with a St Johnstone wine and the appointment of general manager John Litster spurred the launch of the lucrative Saints Super 10 weekly prize draw. Each and every venture was pursued to boost the club coffers.

The unveiling of the new stadium prompted ticket inquiries from a' the airts. McDiarmid Park, rather than the footballing talents of St Johnstone and Clydebank, proved big box office. It was the star of the August 19 show.

The pitch, first sown in the early days of May, and trimmed three times every week from July onwards, was immaculate. Around 25 older fans who had attended the official opening of Muirton Park 65 years previously, enjoyed the occasion as guests of the club. By kick-off, 7,267 customers had eased through the turnstiles.

The opening was kept deliberately low-key, with the razzmatazz reserved for a glamour challenge match with Manchester United come the autumn. Co-operation and understanding was sought from all parties concerned and for fans snarled up in the car park after the match, patience certainly was the all-important virtue. Later, direct access to the nearby by-pass was approved only after persistent lobbying by the club.

Delays were the order of the day. The kick-off was held up eight minutes to accommodate latecomers and, taking the field after the interval, a linesman pulled a muscle. Luckily, local solicitor Graeme Cowper, a qualified official, was on hand to take over after a seven minute lull in the proceedings.

The participants themselves were aware this was history in the making. Grant Jenkins revealed: 'Sammy Johnston and I lined up for the kick-off, but I made sure I got the game going. That's something to tell the grandchildren.

Smart Alex: old friends Ferguson and Totten.

'I came pretty close to hitting the first Saints goal. Jim Hughes took the honours with the first at McDiarmid in seven minutes but it was my header back off the post which let Harry Curran snatch the equaliser.

'If that header had sneaked home I'd have had a double to boast about. I was the last man to score for Saints at Muirton Park, against Partick Thistle on April 8. It was before the cup matches with Rangers and we didn't score in the two remaining games at Perth. I didn't realize that until Steve Maskrey pointed it out. No doubt that will be one for many a pub quiz.'

Victory was sealed via the penalty spot and Don McVicar, 10 minutes from time, with Alex Totten insistent: 'It was important to get off to a winning start. That's true of any season, but this was something special. We had lost our last game at Muirton and the players didn't want to go down in the record books as losers on the opening day at McDiarmid.'

Undefeated in the league, St Johnstone welcomed former player Alex Ferguson and his £12 million Manchester United side to Perth for the official gala opening on the evening of October 17. Totten and Fergie knew each other from their playing days and a call from Perth to the Old Trafford manager's office had set the wheels in motion.

'Manchester United are one of the most glamorous names in world football. In Scotland, ask any kid in the street which English team he supports and you can be pretty certain it will be United or Liverpool. Alex readily agreed to the invitation and it was just a matter of finding a suitable date,' said Totten. 'It was a superb gesture and he brought his full squad north for the occasion.'

Geoff Brown added: 'United indicated two directors would accompany the team, but it was quite a thrill to find Sir Matt Busby and Bobby Charlton had made the trip. Sir Matt has been the perfect ambassador for the game and Scotland. Coming back from the ordeal of the Munich Disaster to mould a European Cup winning team was an incredible achievement. He's a man I admire greatly.'

Like any gala performance, an expectant audience, calculated at 9,780, settled into the seats. Old Trafford guests were introduced during the preliminaries and celebratory fireworks were sent skywards . . . albeit briefly. Within seconds, Scotland keeper Jim Leighton was forced to look lively as a three-foot rocket made an abrupt re-entry in his goalmouth!

Centre stage, the millionaires of Manchester and their hosts quickly dispensed with the formalities, setting about each other with gusto. The friendly tag was overlooked, with Sammy Johnston admitting: 'For the first five minutes they treated it as little more than a training session. Then the tackles started going in and United realised they'd have to take it a bit more seriously!

'I was playing in midfield, up against England skipper Bryan Robson. As a youngster I'd idolised Rangers' Derek Johnstone and, in my teenage years, I'd seen Kenny Dalglish and Robson as the players to admire. Here I was playing against a hero.'

The opening period saw Saints create and fritter away several scoring opportunities. Then came the moment for which the match will forever be remembered. With 32 minutes on the electronic scoreboard, out went the lights. As the emergency generators took over, the scene was reminiscent of an out-take from Close Encounters. Perth referee Doug Yeats assembled the teams in midfield and walked them up the tunnel. It was 20 minutes before he could let battle recommence.

The discomfiture of the moment was recalled by director Douglas McIntyre: 'The lights went out and the chairman turned to me accusingly, to remark "What are you going to do now?" As an electrician, I was the one to bear the brunt of the jokes. But the emergency lights were on within 15 seconds and later the emergency services pointed out how calm everyone had been.

'There was nearly a full house and there was no problem whatsoever. The stadium had been designed to the highest safety specifications and that incident proved it could cope with the unexpected. We could have done without it happening at the gala opening, but the safety aspect was a plus factor.'

Sandwiched between the inevitable welter of substitutions, former Celt Brian McClair snatched the winning goal but the result was of minor consideration on such a night for Perth. Nothing could take the shine off the celebrations.

Alex Ferguson, who paraded record British domestic signing Gary Pallister — a £2.3 million defender whose signature cost the equivalent of two McDiarmid Park stands — and a host of internationals, giving the opening star status, emerged from the dressing room area to tell the waiting media: 'This is the future, the way ahead for all teams. It's a fabulous setting.'

The one-time Aberdeen and Scotland boss lingered to share memories of a Saints hat-trick at Ibrox in a year when only the Muirton side, and Real Madrid did the double over Rangers. He also confessed to having wagered a bob or two on Rangers to win — information he preferred the Press not to part with in the presence of his players that evening! A case, perhaps, of do as I say, not as I do!

The man from Govan impressed all connected with the Perth club by contacting former Muirton stalwart Mrs Mary Gibson who, between 1947 and 1983, filled the role of substitute mother to many a Perth player. A touching private gesture by one of the game's most respected managers, on an evening full of memories and hopes for the future.

That Championship Season

THE most substantial figure ever written out on a St Johnstone cheque to secure the services of a player was the £55,000 accepted by Heart of Midlothian in the summer of 1982, bringing the experience of midfielder Derek Addison from the capital to Muirton Park to spur a challenge for the First Division championship.

But in late May, 1989, the Perth directors agreed to expenditure which engulfed the previous high water mark. Instead of allowing the handsome cash windfall from the sojourn to the Scottish Cup semi-final to accumulate interest in the bank, the manager was given the go-ahead to plan his own investment strategy.

Once again, the First Division championship flag was the ultimate aim and coincidentally, Hearts were again the beneficiaries. Typically, Alex Totten shied away from a speculative venture into the unknown commodities market. For £85,000, Alex Totten knew what he was getting. It's known as a bargain.

Two years earlier, Totten had accompanied Allan Moore and his father on a car journey to Edinburgh which opened the way to full-time football for the promising Dumbarton winger. But word had filtered through that the Edinburgh club would not be difficult to deal with.

Moore's first-team experience ran to 48 matches, including a man of the match accolade in a European tie with Austria Vienna. But for much of his time at Tynecastle, he was forced to play the role of reluctant understudy to John Colquhoun. They were from much the same mould.

Colquhoun left Celtic Park in search of first-team football, after living in the shadow of Davie Provan. And that same desire for the limelight, rather than the chorus line, prompted Moore's departure from the Gorgie Road.

Sammy Johnston in full flight.

Explained Totten: 'The first thing I did was bring Allan to Perth. We went straight to McDiarmid Park because I wanted to show the player what this club was all about. It was a bit of psychology, because I had to convince him it was a wise career move. With a wife and family to support, Allan was wary of stepping back to part-time football. It wasn't an easy decision but one look at the stadium underlined the ambitious nature of the club. I knew I could use my contacts to arrange a job outside the game. In many ways, it was rather like my own decision to come to Saints. It was a question of taking one step backwards to advance in the long-term.

'I knew we were talking about a record transfer fee for St Johnstone but I had no qualms about that. It was much the same price Hearts had paid to Dumbarton and Allan had gained two years of experience as a full-time footballer. I knew his background and his qualities — and his typical Glasgow patter was just the thing for dressing room morale.'

At 24 years of age, with a wife, baby daughter and mortgage responsibilities, Moore had some thinking to do before turning away from full-time football. It dominated his waking hours for the next seven days. He explained: 'I wasn't keen to turn part-time but McDiarmid Park made all the difference to my attitude. To be honest, I thought Muirton was a bit of a dump but one look at the new stadium proved the club was ambitious. That was enough to convince me where my future lay.'

He of the cheeky grin and nature to match, had once attracted more illustrious names than St Johnstone with his waltzes on the wing. As a precocious 21-year-old, he joined two other starry-eyed lads with their hearts set on bidding a fond farewell to Dumbarton and saying bonjour to 'Le Football Francais.'

'St Etienne were a big club and had links with Michel Platini. On a four day trip, we were jumping around a hotel room, hugging each other and doing somersaults, thinking we had signed. We couldn't believe it — we shouldn't have believed it! The next thing, we read in the paper that the deal was off. That was a real sickener. It was my first chance at a big move and I don't mind admitting I was crying.'

In pre-season Saints played a closed-doors friendly with Rangers at The Albion training ground and his new manager admitted: 'Allan's spell at Hearts had made a tremendous difference. There was no question this was money well spent. Right away, I knew he would be influential in taking the club to the Premier League. His pace was electric and he was a crowd pleaser — a marvellous combination.'

Next in the door at McDiarmid Park was midfield man Harry Curran, making the 22-mile journey from Tannadice for around £50,000. Curran, surprise, surprise, also figured in Totten's sphere of influence at Dumbarton before Dundee United offered full-time terms. Unlike Moore, he needed little convincing to step back into the part-time ranks.

'At Boghead, Harry had played in a variety of positions. He was actually a left-back when he signed for United, but I knew he could play in defence, midfield or attack if required,' said Totten. 'After our showing the previous season, I knew the championship was a genuine possibility if the squad could be strengthened.

'Just as I knew what Harry could do for St Johnstone, he was aware of my expectations. I know it took the fans some time to warm to the player, but later they were won over when the benefit of full-time training became apparent. There was no doubt Harry suffered, like Allan later that season, from being restricted to training on a part-time basis.'

The player put pen to paper on the eve of the season, and made

Steve Maskrey
takes a bow.

his debut in a one goal win at Alloa only after the manager, who had signed an extended contract of his own through to June 1992, made a morning dash to Glasgow with appropriate registration forms.

'I had been at Tannadice for more than two years and it was time for a change. I wanted a clean break from United, where first team appearances had been few and far between,' said Curran. 'With plans for marriage, I was keen to return home to live in Glasgow and I knew I could pick up my old job with a glazing firm. I didn't have to think twice about the move to Perth.'

While Curran was donning the blue and white working gear, others were proving more reticent. Gary Thompson, Tommy Coyle and Steve Maskrey had declined, for one reason or another, to commit themselves to the cause as Saints headed over the border for a brief tour taking in Shrewsbury and Manchester.

Coyle, a joiner to trade, found difficulty with the Perth training schedule and a £15,000 fee met his desire for a West Coast club. In September, he joined up with brother Owen at Clydebank and Saints netted an extra three grand on their purchase price. Gary Thompson, now 33, departed for Forfar before the turn of the year, with £5,000 changing hands. He had played 66 games over a two-year period and his contribution to the Perth club's resurrection was considerable.

The Maskrey wrangle was a different matter. A combination of a natural desire for full-time football and a row rooted in bonus payments for the Rangers semi-final put the striker, who shared Player of the Year accolades with Paul Cherry, at odds with the club. He missed the first 10 games of the season before a contract was extended through to the summer.

'Steve trained at Blackburn — just as Mark Treanor was later to visit Fulham — and their Perth-born manager Don Mackay advised him to go back to training with Saints and put himself in the shop window. He was assured we wouldn't stand in his way if the right offer came along,' said Totten.

The previous term's most prolific strike star, Maskrey admitted to disillusionment but inisted that a point of principle, as much as cash, was the bone of contention. In fact, as the dispute dragged on, he was seriously pursuing the prospect of plying his trade in Australia.

'When I went to Blackburn, I was still having trouble with the knee injured six months before. Finally, a compromise was worked out which suited both the manager and myself. Things worked out well after that.'

The Skol Cup brought a lengthy trip to Dumfries to face a Queen of the South side demoted from the First Division with a miserly 10 points to their credit. The return journey seemed even longer. A penalty goal gave home fans their first cause for celebration since November.

Harry Curran, making only his second appearance for Saints, admitted: 'That was a terrible night. Everyone was rank rotten! I didn't really know the boys and the atmosphere on the bus home was horrible. But from the previous three training sessions I'd seen enough to suggest there were quality players at Perth and promotion was a genuine possibility.'

Totten confessed: 'I went berserk that night. We didn't play

The crucial strike: Mark Treanor slots home the penalty equaliser in the Airdrie classic.

individually or collectively. It brought the side back to earth with an almighty thump. Maybe it was just the shot they needed, because we set off on a superb run in the league.'

Allan Moore's impact was immediate, with a hat-trick against Forfar, and the winger notched another goal as Saints topped the table with a splendid 2-0 win at Kirkcaldy hallmarked by one of their most exhilarating opening 45 minutes of the year. When full-time Hamilton, relegated from the upper flight, were trounced by three at Perth, the fans began to think talk of promotion was more than idle banter.

No one could recall a more positive start to the season and the new McDiarmid turnstiles clicked faster than any others in the First Division. On the transfer front, an exchange deal with Alloa saw the departure of John Irvine and the arrival of Billy Blackie, a one-time colleague of Roddy Grant. Stuart Sorbie went to Raith Rovers for £18,000 and Forfar's leading scorer, Kenny Ward, came to Perth for £20,000.

'With only one team being promoted to the Premier League, we knew it was going to be tough,' said Totten. 'But our cup performance against Rangers injected tremendous self-belief. An awful lot of people thought we would be slaughtered in the first match and our display convinced the players they could beat any side in the First Division.

'The fans responded in strength. The new stadium and the accompanying hype attracted the curious, but we were giving them the kind of attacking football they wanted to see. We went 15 league games undefeated before losing 2-1 to Airdrie in November. I couldn't have asked for a better start to the promotion campaign.'

At Ayr, Saints looked set to lose their proud record, having already lost Mark Treanor to a red card. Two goals up, Ally's army found itself depleted by a double departure; Kenny Ward pulled one back, two minutes from the end McVicar hammered home a penalty equaliser, and still there was time for Don to miss a spot-kick!

But the match-up the media wanted was pencilled in for October 30, with Partick Thistle and Chic Charnley, darling of the Glasgow scribes, on a run of 25 matches without defeat. It stirred the imagination of both sets of fans and all 10,169 seats were sold. An all-ticket First Division match — a phenomenon so rare the BBC came to town — and no one was short-changed.

When the smoke cleared, the referee had a wee black book to match anything Warren Beattie could muster. There were nine yellow cards flourished and an ordering off — John Dempsey departing for crudely bringing goalscorer Allan Moore back to earth. Moore's forehead flicked Saints into the lead and sustained pressure culminated in an 87th minute Maskrey strike. Partick's consolation counter was reserved for an inconsequential penalty from Charnley. The Perth advantage stretched to four points on a day of drama when McDiarmid Park edged towards accumulated crowds of 60,000.

The triumph over Partick delighted one Saints supporter in particular. There were 13 envelopes each containing £25 waiting for the players at reception. It wasn't the only indication that the players were winning over the fans. A pre-Christmas evening out at Glasgow's Grosvenor Hotel came courtesy of a cheque from an elderly Aberfeldy gentleman.

Saints were back in the news. The only unbeaten team in the United Kingdom, a stadium complimented by Lord Justice Taylor . . . and John Embleton's run-in with the forces of law and order. The Perth club's youngest fan, at only five months, fell foul of the Scottish Criminal Justice Act 1980 when police branded his baby's bottle 'a sealed container'. The offending object was taken into custody, the Press pounced and a front page headline gleefully trumpeted: 'The Milky Barred Kid'.

Steve Maskrey shoots Saints towards the title at Ayr.

Allan Moore, a B and Q Super Skills monthly award winner, was also gobbling up the column inches. Defenders were doling out their own brand of punishment and retaliation late in a game against Albion Rovers attracted a four match ban, ruling the striker out of the vital Airdrie engagement.

The player himself recalled: 'I was getting fed up with players kicking me and I retaliated. I was attracting a lot of publicity for a First Division player and maybe some opposition teams were saying: "Who does he think he is?" There were some nasty kicks but I don't think the markers were malicious. Maybe I was just that bit quicker. Retaliation was silly and the manager didn't half let me know about it. It was stupid and I let myself down. I missed crucial matches and I don't think I fully recovered my sharpness after suspension.'

Totten noted: 'Allan was on the receiving end of some rough treatment as defenders tried to stop him any way they could. Every week, he was the target for someone having a go. On one occasion three different opponents were booked for fouling him. But the player knew retaliation was foolish.'

Further troubles followed when defender Alan McKillop, returning to the fray two operations and 14 frustrating months later, walked out on the club after being dropped. Believing he had been made a scapegoat for defensive troubles, McKillop warned he was ready to give up the game. After a loan period with Arbroath, he finally moved to Brechin.

'Alan felt he wasn't getting a fair crack of the whip when I brought back Paul Cherry to partner Kenny Thomson in central defence. It was unfortunate, because Alan had a marvellous season when he came out of the Second Division. He thoroughly deserved his Player of the Year awards and was very unfortunate with injury,' said Totten.

As 1989 drew to a close, St Johnstone were setting the pace, still undefeated on their travels. Then, on December 30, the wheels fell off the bandwagon. Clydebank, with Owen Coyle (later a £175,000 target for promotion rivals Airdrie) and Ken Eadie rampant, dispensed a four goal humiliation. Perth fans trooped home disconsolately nursing a premature Hogmanay hangover. It was the heaviest league defeat since Totten took command.

Fortunately, the effects didn't linger and the perfect New Year pick-me-up came in the form of a 5-1 derby win at Forfar. But a home defeat from Raith Rovers, marred by another early exit for Allan Moore, bumped Saints off their top of the table perch. It made a January trip to Firhill all the more precarious.

Mark Treanor, whose mischievous sense of humour was emphasised by a programme note listing his favourite actors as Al Pacino and former colleague Owen Coyle, was the centre of attention. He had first crack at the bathwater after clashing with Chic Charnley, but only after striking home a penalty winner. The margin might have been slim but the result effectively reduced the championship race to a head-to-head dual with Jimmy Bone's Airdrie. Partick now trailed nine points behind.

The Scottish Cup threw up another date with Rangers, now further bolstered by the likes of big money signings Trevor Steven, Maurice Johnston and Nigel Spackman. The bookies didn't fancy Saints chances one little bit, offering speculators odds of 14-1. Within three minutes, even those prices looked miserly, as Johnston whipped the opener past John Balavage.

'Having been at Ibrox, I knew the last thing we could afford was an early slip,' recalled Totten. 'Rangers went on to win easily with goals from John Brown and Mark Walters. But with a 39,000 crowd, it provided another welcome money spinner and, in

Going up: Saints in civvies at Ayr.

retrospect, the defeat wasn't such a bad thing. It meant we could concentrate all our attention on the league.'

Talking to Pressmen flanked by the glittering prizes of the Ibrox trophy room, the Perth manager revealed an experienced hand was being lined-up to join the crew taking the club towards their stated destination: the Premier League. Within hours, and with 14 games remaining, 35-year-old Paul Hegarty was a Saint.

A model professional, Hegarty was the most experienced player ever to play for the Perth club. Sixty-eight European football appearances, seven international caps and Premier championship memories were all part of the package. In his testimonial year with Dundee United, the free transfer deal included an agreement to train on a full-time basis at Tannadice.

Totten explained the surprise move: 'Paul brought charisma. The players were well aware of his achievements and looked up to him. His record spoke for itself and his arrival gave us a tremendous boost at a crucial time in the promotion battle.'

Totten turned again to Tannadice for his next signing. This time, the cost of the signature took St Johnstone Football Club into uncharted territory. For the first time, a £100,000 player was on the books. Gary McGinnis, at 26, made his debut at full-back in a February defeat at Brockville. A former team-mate of Harry Curran, he, like Hegarty, continued to enjoy full-time status.

'After nine years with United, without breaking through into the first team on a regular basis, I'd had enough. It was a great club, revered throughout Europe during the earlier part of the eighties, but I wanted to prove I could be more than just a handy squad man,' said McGinnis, who had reluctantly covered for internationalists like Paul Hegarty, David Narey and Maurice Malpas.

'I'd already asked away from United, and that meant the punishment of afternoon training on my own. I was going stale and felt degraded because my ability wasn't seen as being worthy of a regular game by the manager. Yet, when I was called in, I don't think I ever let him down.

'In fact, when Jim McLean called to say Saints wanted me, he revealed I was in his plans for the weekend game! But I was doing cartwheels in the house the minute the phone went down. After all those years of frustration at Tannadice it felt like freedom was beckoning. It was an incredible feeling.

'Saints were doing well and at last I had a chance to prove myself. The fact that I could continue to live in the Tayside area was an added bonus. Continuing to train at Tannadice was fine because I got on well with the players and staff. But I'd always believed I was good enough to merit a run in the team.

'The manager had praised me when I'd come in but I wasn't prepared to settle for being known as a squad player who would always give 100 per cent. It annoyed me that I'd play well against the Old Firm or Aberdeen but miss out on the next match because one of the regulars was fit again. The Saints move was perfect for me.'

Once again, the directors had backed the manager, courtesy of the Scottish Cup proceeds. No one could accuse the board of penny-pinching at this crucial stage of the club's development. In a turn-of-the-year interview, chairman Geoff Brown reacted to a whispering campaign suggesting the club would not be too distraught to trail Airdrie home to the finishing line.

He insisted: 'I'm not used to being second in anything. If I honestly didn't think we could do better than second, I wouldn't be here. I believe there are winners and losers in life. If you adopt a positive attitude you will win more than you lose, and I think we have a winning set-up at McDiarmid Park.

'Everybody connected with this club wants to see it competing at the highest possible level — and that must mean the Premier League.'

Champions! Don McVicar takes the trophy.

The emphasis was on the word competing and a £350,000 strategy, not inclusive of new players, was mapped out to bring back full-time football to Perth if their mission was accomplished.

But with all eyes firmly focussed on an impending McDiarmid Park face-to-face with the Broomfield frontrunners, Saints seemed set to flop against lowly Albion Rovers. Two goals down, the championship looked a forlorn hope. But, spurred on by a loyal and vociferous support, they mounted an extraordinary salvage operation with Paul Cherry the hero. Four goals in the closing 10 minutes hauled Saints back into contention.

Defender Mark Treanor noted that Cliftonhill, on a damp, dreich afternoon, wasn't the most inspirational of backdrops: 'But at least there was atmosphere created by the visiting fans. It's certainly not the worst place to play. I remember, with Clydebank, we travelled to Meadowbank and the manager's tactics talk had to compete with piped music — Tom Jones blasting out 'Delilah' over the dressing room sound system! In those days, it was like turning up to play a game of five-a-side with your mates. It's changed now, but there still isn't much in the way of atmosphere about the place.'

The weekend after that inspirational fightback, downwardly mobile Alloa were hit for six, quickly followed by a slim, and late, win at Hamilton. The scene was set for the showdown. On March 31, 1989, Airdrie came to town for the match of the season.

The Diamonds, with a one-point advantage and a game in hand, had lost only once in 18 outings. No wonder the sell-out signs were posted at McDiarmid Park. As the *Perthshire Advertiser* back page blared, truly this was: The Big One.

Four years after Totten's arrival in Perth, the prospects of Premier League football were going on the line. It was win or bust for Saints. Every single one of the record 9,556 spectators who crammed the Crieff Road stadium knew they were playing for high stakes. The entire season, future seasons, the hopes and aspirations of both clubs: all would be shaped by the outcome of the next 90 minutes.

The sun was shining on the shirt-sleeved crowd, paying around £40,000 for the privilege, as the show got under way. It was pure theatre, a classic confrontation, Scotland's match of the season — demanding a special place in many a video collection.

Maskrey rattled the crossbar early on, a goal-line escape inspired Airdrie keeper John Martin, Cherry and Grant touched wood . . . but still no luck for cavalier Saints. The pressure pounded down on the Airdrie defence and Owen Coyle, Scotland's top scorer, was starved of possession. Surely it was just a matter of time before the breakthrough?

Then, in 69 minutes, Stevie Gray, a £70,000 buy from Aberdeen, raged a drive past John Balavage in a rare Airdrie venture upfield. The north stand erupted, a cauldron of red and white. If this was a clash of the heavyweights, it looked like a knock-out sucker punch had been delivered.

Recalling the anguish of the moment, Paul Cherry, whose Player of the Year collection was to swell with another seven statuettes coming his way, conceded: 'Everything we had played for seemed to be collapsing. Back in August, we genuinely thought we could take the title and as the months passed, the first result the players looked for was Airdrie's. We all knew this game was going to have a crucial bearing on the future of both clubs.

'When that opening goal went in, after all the pressure we had exerted, I remember falling to my knees. The whole season was

That championship feeling.

disintegrating. But the fighting spirit throughout the team was incredible. We were patient and battled back into contention. It's by far the best game of football I've ever played in. That game had everything, absolutely everything.'

Keeper Balavage recalled glancing towards the electronic scoreboard, forlornly deciding the fates were conspiring against the Saints. His opposite number seemed capable of turning back the blue tidal wave all afternoon and, with time against the Perth side, the championship seemed bound for Broomfield.

But not for the first time that season, Saints hauled themselves up off the deck, like a weary prize fighter operating on remote control and personal pride. With Heddle and Ward replacing an exhausted McGinnis and Johnston ('I was carrying an injury and probably shouldn't have played, but it was just too big a game to miss out on'), Airdrie were driven back into their defensive shell. Maskrey jinked into the box, down he went . . . penalty! Mark Treanor, the coolest man in the place, slammed home the equaliser. Fourteen minutes left. 'It was the most important penalty kick I'd ever taken, whether for Clydebank or Saints. If I'd missed it the heads would have gone down. In fact, mine might have rolled! But, in all honesty, at the time I wasn't thinking about that,' said the man of the moment. 'Playing at full-back, I'm just happy to get into the box and have a free shot at goal. It doesn't happen very often!

'I know some players don't fancy taking penalty kicks but the main thing is to make up you're mind what you're going to do, and stick with it. It's a question of confidence and I'd only missed one previously. In fact, I made up my mind where I was going to place it the previous evening.'

Treanor revealed that he'd been watching a preview of the game on a Friday sports programme. It included a look back at the penalty he converted earlier in the year to put paid to Partick Thistle's promotion prospects.

'I decided that if I was watching it, Airdrie keeper John Martin might be tuned in as well. I made up my mind that if there was a penalty, I would send it towards the other corner. I don't know if the television influenced John, but he went the wrong way.'

Harry Curran, consigned to the dug-out with a stomach injury, insisted: 'Airdrie went ahead with that wonder goal from Stevie Gray, but somehow we knew it was going to be our day. You could sense it in the stadium, there was a belief that we could come back, not just to draw but to win.'

The draw was tailor-made for the league leaders, and it showed in the shape of the game. But, with only four minutes remaining, Roddy Grant headed super Saints in the direction of the Premier League, connecting with Treanor's driven free-kick. A cult hero with the fans, man-of-the-match Roddy notched 19 goals in this championship season — but none as valuable as this. It helped consolidate a B and Q Skills Award for April.

'I'd set myself a target of 20 goals for the season and it was disappointing not to hit the mark, although it was the best total I'd achieved. But that was number 17 and it was a wee bit special. Definitely the most important goal I'd scored all season,' said the Gloucester-born leader of the line. 'The fans certainly enjoyed it, because there had been an extra edge of rivalry with Airdrie all season.'

With the full-time opposition devastated, the Saints subs combined to inflict the coup de grace, Ward dispatching Heddle's measured cross in the final minute. The standing ovation was richly deserved. The impact of this result reverberated over subsequent weeks.

Despondent Airdrie manager Jimmy Bone, to his credit, sportingly admitted: 'We were badly outplayed. We have no complaints.' Totten — Scottish Brewers' manager of the month — cautioned his players: 'We have achieved nothing yet. There are five games to go and Airdrie can still pip us.'

Victory, again, at Firhill stretched the Perth advantage to three points, as Airdrie stumbled at Clydebank. But the Bankies left Perth with a 3-1 win and Clyde departed with a point as nerves on and off the park were stretched to the limit. But the Diamonds couldn't recover their sparkle after the defeat at Perth. As Totten said: 'We destroyed them psychologically that day. They simply had no answer — there was no way back.'

On April 28, 1990, Totten addressed his troops at the Towans Hotel, Prestwick — an establishment owned by former Rangers goalkeeper Norrie Martin and a favourite stopping place for Saints before appointments in Ayr.

He recalled: 'I told them now was the time to be positive. The championship was there for the taking and all season they had proved they were a team to be reckoned with. We could expect no favours, but this was what we had played for — a chance to win the title.'

More than 5,000, maybe more than 6,000 (whatever attendance figure favoured, the bulk unquestionably hailed from Perthshire) filed into Somerset Park to see if Saints could secure their first title flag since Alex Rennie restored Premier League football to Perth in 1983. A young entrepreneur did very nicely, enticing the optimists to invest in banners emblazoned: 'Champions'. Another reported brisk business with t-shirts in much the same vein.

Derby-born Paul Cherry, with only three goals from the previous 38 outings, picked out his fourth with an immaculate sense of timing. The champagne had been packed, but only a breath-taking penalty save from John Balavage, en route to 16 shut-outs, prevented it staying on ice.

'Without doubt that was the most important single save of my career. I had an idea where the ball was going and it was struck well, but I stretched a finger tip to it,' said the man of the moment. Any suggestion he may have moved early was met in equally agile fashion: 'I may have been leaning that way. Blame it on poor balance!'

Then, with 32 minutes still to play, Steve Maskrey pounced for goal number 12. The man who had begun the season out in the cold warmed the hearts of the Perth support. Cue the celebrations!

'The scenes on the final whistle were incredible. The players rushed together in the centre-circle, hugging each other and applauding the fans,' said Totten. 'I headed round the track — I wanted to thank each and every one of the fans personally if I could. I spotted one of our schoolboy signings Steven Smith, from Blairgowrie, with his father and he walked around the ground with me. It's a day neither of us will forget.'

Back in the dressing room, mayhem reigned supreme. Paul Hegarty professed the thrill matched his Premier title win with Dundee United; the champagne corks threatened the well-being of the photographers; and the good vibrations from the raucous songs of victory threatened to impinge upon the Richter Scale.

Messrs Totten and Paton were flung unceremoniously into the bath. In the heat of the moment, no one had thought to dip an elbow to ascertain the temperature — and the duo were lucky to escape third degree burns as they emerged hot and flustered, to undiluted pandemonium!

'Somerset Park had one of the few remaining communal baths in Scottish football and it was left to the players to add cold water to reach the desired temperature,' said Bertie Paton. 'We were thrown in fully clothed. Luckily, I landed on my feet and balanced on my hands for an instant. I don't think I've ever moved so fast in my life!'

After a brief cooling off period, Totten recalled: 'I remember settling the players, but, to be honest, I broke down in tears. Emotion got the better of me. I told them the highlight of my career had been walking up the Marble Staircase to become assistant manager of Rangers, but it didn't match this. Taking a team of my own to the Premier League was the greatest moment of all. I was proud of each and every one of the squad.'

The Towans Hotel hosted the victory soiree and the celebrations continued beyond the midnight hour. Totten maintained: 'The adrenalin was still flowing. It had been a very special day for everyone connected with the club — the directors, the players and the fans. Many of the players said it was the best

Showing off the silverware.

night of their lives. Willie Thornton once told me that in football one pleasant memory was worth a thousand dreams. It's a quote I've used before — but it still holds true. That day was very special indeed.'

St Johnstone's efforts were appreciated further afield: before the commencement of hostilities, one Leeds United fan had wagered more than a few bob on the Perth club and a championship treble, in tandem with his own favourites and Liverpool. Around £130,000 helped cure his summertime blues!

Seven days later, the Perth club hosted their own championship party and nearly 8,000 guests entered into the spirit of the occasion. Captain Don McVicar remained sidelined, a victim of suspension, and the threat of another caution and subsequent ban kept Allan Moore in civvies. That gave 19-year-old David Bingham a memorable league debut chance. Totten explained: 'I wanted to make sure Allan was available for the start of the new season. I did exactly the same when we were promoted from the Second Division, dropping Doug Barron and Alan McKillop.'

Moore was less than enchanted with the managerial directive: 'Looking back on it, he was quite right. But it was very disappointing to miss out on that match. The manager told me he didn't want me picking up another booking and sitting out the first four matches in the Premier League.'

The match itself, with Forfar visiting, was simply a preliminary to the Main Event: the presentation of the championship. Roddy Grant created the right party mood with a 69th minute goal to secure Saints 25th league win and a four-point advantage on Airdrie. The Association of Football Statisticians were later to hail Saints as the country's top team, with a 75 per cent success rate leaving Rangers and Liverpool trailing.

'That was our 81st League goal of the season,' said Totten. 'Only Tranmere in the English Third Division, scored more than us — but they played seven more fixtures. St Johnstone were the highest scoring side in Scotland and that gave the fans enormous satisfaction. It proved we were a team dedicated to attacking football. We won the title without being negative, although we did concede fewer goals than anyone else in the division.'

Yule Craig, vice-president of the Scottish League, presented McVicar with the championship trophy and the silverware, once thought likely to prove more elusive than the Holy Grail, was hoisted above assorted heads.

For McVicar, it was an especially poignant moment. It was his second championship with Saints but suspension had forced him into a spectating role for the last four matches. He explained: 'I felt honoured when the manager asked me to accept the trophy as club captain. Paul Hegarty had been filling the role and I wouldn't have been at all surprised if he had been given the chance to do the honours. The cup semi-final matches with Rangers were memorable but accepting that championship was definitely the highlight of my Saints career up to that point.'

The Reserve League East title also came to McDiarmid Park, with the young Saints and coach Tommy Campbell deservedly sharing the attention. That night, the tills of many a local hostelry rang to the tunes of glory. There were a few 'sarry heids' ushered in with the Sabbath, but none more so than young David Bingham's. Larking around in the dressing room, he was felled by a blow-up plastic champagne bottle. Curiously his assailant was Allan Moore, the man left out of proceedings!

'The bottle was thrown onto the park during the lap of honour.

I cracked Davie over the head, and he needed six stitches! I didn't realise the base was solid. It was a complete accident but the players said different, of course. Mind you, it put him in his place!'

Saints championship achievement didn't go unnoticed by Perth and Kinross District Council and, in an unprecedented move, an open-top bus tour of the Fair City was arranged before a civic reception at the Old City Chambers. Thousands of blue and white draped families turned out on street corners to salute their heroes. Even the drizzle didn't dampen their delight and the lap of honour was extended to 90 minutes.

Crowds thronged the High Street and Perth and District Pipe Band welcomed the champions, flanked by police outriders. The city had never witnessed anything quite like it. Provost Alex Murray paid tribute to everyone involved 'in bringing St Johnstone back to life' and joined club personnel taking a bow on the balcony.

'It was another wonderful night for everyone connected with the club. The players had their wives and girlfriends with them, and I felt that was important,' said the manager. 'Football can be a selfish game and it was good for them to share in the success.

'In 1968 I remember being on a tour of Dunfermline after the club won the Scottish Cup, and it seemed like half of Fife had turned out for the occasion. We didn't know what to expect in Perth, especially with the weather turning bad. We needn't have worried — the reception was incredible.'

The First Division championship was the first tangible sign of success for the McDiarmid Park tophy cabinet. Saints were marching proudly into the Premier League — but that could wait for tomorrow. The evening of May 8, 1990, was for reflection and basking in the glory of a job well done.

The Survival Strategy

ST JOHNSTONE, observers were agreed, had been promoted to the 'relegation zone' of the Premier League. Even the announcement that full-time football was returning to Perth after a gap of 14 years, with manager Alex Totten putting pen to paper for three years, did little to dissuade the doubters in the Scottish game.

If the money was piling onto champions Rangers to retain their title, precious little went behind the Premier League newcomers, even at prices of 500-1. The two previous excursions into the big boys' playground had ended with noses bloodied and pride severely dented.

One enterprising emporium in Perth tempted speculation by quoting Saints at 8-1 for the title, but there was no danger of a speculators' stampede, even allowing for a 30-point advantage on the scratch favourites before a ball was kicked in earnest.

As it turned out, all the clever money was being invested by the McDiarmid club during those summer months. If Saints had scaled a mountain to grasp the First Division championship, surely they faced a task of Everest-like proportions simply to secure a foothold in the Premier League?

No one at the Perth club was harbouring any illusions. St Johnstone had wrestled themselves free from the clutches of creditors to enjoy financial independence and coveted membership of the soccer elite in four memorable years. The manager had only three seasons under his belt. But an extended stay in the company of the country's Top Ten provided a challenge to relish.

'On several occasions during the promotion winning season, the manager approached the board requesting full-time football

The Premier Club.

for several players, say four or five. In fact, the signings of Gary
McGinnis and Paul Hegarty showed the path the club was
taking,' said Geoff Brown. 'We were extremely grateful to the
Tannadice club for their co-operation, in allowing both players to
continue training with their former colleagues.

'Many of the players who clinched the title had helped us out of
the Second Division, but there had to be a realistic assessment of
their prospects of competing in the Premier League. The club had
to turn full-time to have any chance in the top grade. In fact, the
directors had decided to go for the full-time option even if we
missed out on promotion.

'Crowd figures virtually doubled with the move to McDiarmid
Park. The board opted to generate cash which, ultimately, paid
for the players attracted to Perth before the start of the Premier
season. Had we gone full-time earlier that would not have been
possible.'

Brown explained that the manager, when he arrived at the club,
was told to identify players likely to strengthen St Johnstone. It
would be left to the board to take any further action. The
relationship between manager and chairman was to follow the
continental example, with Brown and his colleagues taking care of
transfer transactions.

'Liverpool handle this the correct way. Why should a football
manager be asked to negotiate contracts, wages, signing-on fees
and the like? It's totally alien territory for men who've lived their
lives within a football framework. It's not fair to ask a manager to

take on these responsibilities. It won't be long before most clubs in Scotland follow the way of the Europeans, with managers concentrating on coaching responsibilities.

'At no time is the manager answerable to the board for team selection. We don't tell him who to put in or who to leave out of the side. But when it comes to spending the club's money, that's a different matter. It's our responsibility to make sure it's being spent wisely and, as I've always maintained, the financial stability of St Johnstone will not be undermined in the transfer market.

'I remember a previous director warning me that footballers were a different breed for a boss to handle. My answer to that was "Have you ever tried dealing with squads of bricklayers?" But, in retrospect, I should have listened to him!'

'Football has its priorities all wrong. The financial predicament so many clubs now face underlines that simple fact. Sensible people under pressure to produce results from the fans, media and management approve expenditure they would never contemplate in their own line of business.

'The directors of St Johnstone Football Club are as passionate about the team as any supporter but the ship must be kept on an even keel. The football team doesn't come first, the football club does. Coming into St Johnstone, the priority was survival — and no one ever wants to see that again.'

For several of the squad which had walked the glory road with Saints, it was the end of the line. Exemplary veteran Ken Thomson, the oldest outfield player in professional football at 38 and without a suspension to his name, negotiated a deal with Cowdenbeath. Other free transfers went to keeper Jim Butter and fellow reserves Willie Newbigging, Scott Ferguson, David Martin and Gary Maher. The open to transfer list included Grant Jenkins, Mike Smith, Billy Blackie and Alan McKillop. Paul Hegarty left for the managerial post at Forfar.

Alex Totten vividly remembers the day Merseyside legend Bill Shankly called him to his Anfield office to inform the teenager his future lay elsewhere: 'Of course it was bitter pill to swallow. But he told me to my face. It's never pleasant telling players they're not part of the club's plans for the next season but it's part and parcel of a manager's job. It's not something that can be shirked.

'When Saints left the Second Division, several players found

Lindsay Hamilton changes the hue of his blue.

themselves victims of their own success. It was exactly the same when we won the Division One title. Players come and players go, it's as simple as that. The squad which did so well at that level wasn't going to survive in the Premier League.

'Full-time football was essential. We had to match our rivals in terms of fitness, tactical awareness and preparation if we were to have any chance of survival. But, as the team being promoted, it was only natural to be cast as red-hot favourites to go back down again.'

Assistant Bertie Paton welcomed an end to the frustrations of three hours weekly training with part-time players: 'In those circumstances coaching is a joke. It's more a question of keeping them ticking over between games. Now, we can take players aside and improve their skills. The next step I'd favour would be having the players live locally.

'I'd like to see players working harder on their game in Scotland. On one of Andy Roxburgh's visits to Italy he took in an A.C. Milan training session and found class international players were ready and willing to work at the skill factor. Footballers don't appreciate how lucky they are until their playing days are drawing to a close. That's the way it's always been. Alex and I keep telling them they have a fabulous life and to make the most of it before it disappears.'

Players like Doug Barron, the longest serving man on the books, John Balavage and Ian Heddle, declined the full-time package on offer. All three accepted this was the obvious track for the club to pursue into the Premier League and, in restricting their training commitment to the standard Tuesday and Thursday evening sessions, they were destined for the periphery of the managerial selection frame.

As it turned out, Balavage retained possession of the keeper's jersey when the new season began in earnest. But he appreciated the writing was on the wall when he shied away from the terms offered. As he explained: 'Full-time football wasn't for me, at my age with family responsibilities and a steady, secure signalling engineer's job with the railway. Had the opportunity come earlier in my career at Perth I would have thought long and hard about the offer. But with a family and mortgage commitments I couldn't afford to take the gamble. The injury possibilities also figured at the back of my mind in that respect.'

Doug Barron, also nearing 30, pointed to a career with a computer disc drive firm, and his 'mature years' for declining the full-time contract: 'I'd have jumped at the chance in my younger years. But it wouldn't have been a wise move, and later signings proved I made the right decision.'

For Ian Heddle, at 27, it was a different matter: 'If at that stage, there had been a safety net ensuring more than one season in the Premier League I would have gone for the full-time option. As things turned out, it proved to be a major mistake and one I'll

Medallion man, Saints Sergei.

always regret. I'm not self-confident by nature and harboure(doubts if I was good enough to perform at that level.

'Later, the odd game I did play convinced me I'd over-rated the standard in the Premier League. It wasn't as demanding as I'd imagined it would be. I think all the talk of internationals, million pound players and foreign signings undermined confidence in my own ability. It was one of those decisions you just have to live with and there's no point in falling victim to what-might-have-beens.

'Football can be a wicked game. Players are forgotten quickly but I've no hard feelings. I enjoyed a whirlwind four years coming up through the divisions and it was great just being part of it all.'

Fans' favourite Paul Cherry committed himself to the club, but only in circumstances tinged with sorrow. The lure of a professional career in football was intense, but with his wife, Nicola, expecting twins, insurance in Edinburgh looked a safer employment bet than football in Perth.

'For the sake of my family, I didn't think it would be fair to gamble by going full-time,' said Cherry. 'I was aware the fans were wondering why I hadn't signed but it was a difficult time for us. We lost the twins and that changed my outlook on life completely. Suddenly full-time football made sense. It gave us the opportunity of a fresh start, we could live in Perth and it meant I would have more time to spend with my wife and children, Nicholas and Christopher. That swung the balance and made it an attractive proposition.'

With the Perth directors approving an investment programme unprecedented in club history, Alex Totten turned to Ibrox for his first recruit. Lindsay Hamilton had been the first Scot signed by Graeme Souness on his arrival in Govan, with £50,000 swelling the coffers of Stenhousemuir. But the imposing goalkeeper found his understudy role to England international Chris Woods usurped by Israeli cap Bonni Ginzburg.

'Jock Wallace and I had eyed Lindsay during our period with Rangers. All he needed was the opportunity to prove what he could do at the top level. We were offering him a chance at Premier Division football every week,' explained Totten.

Hamilton freely admitted he had something to prove, both to himself and to people within the game. The nearest he flirted with a place in the Ibrox first eleven was a bench berth in European competition. His capabilities were never put to the test in the Premier League.

'Anyone born and bred in Scotland and playing football here wants to make the grade at the highest level. That means the Premier League and, in goalkeeping terms, a host of internationalists like Eire's Pat Bonner, Scotland's Andy Goram and Theo Snelders, who has played for Holland.

'Within myself, I still feel I was capable of doing a job for Rangers. Coming from the West of Scotland, everything is orientated towards Rangers and Celtic and maybe, had I been a teenager, the stress of being labelled a reject might have been too much.'

The indisputable low point of his period on the Ibrox payroll came before an early season Skol Cup tie involving Arbroath in a visit to Glasgow. With automatic number one choice Chris

Woods sidelined by a shoulder injury sustained in the opening league encounter with St Mirren, Hamilton was briefed and mentally prepared for a long-awaited debut.

'I was part of the pre-match team talks at a hotel in Glasgow, my family were in the stand to see the game — but when I arrived at the ground, I discovered Bonni Ginzburg was playing. He didn't even have a work permit and that later attracted a fine for Rangers,' said Hamilton. 'That hurt, I can assure you. Hopefully nothing remotely like it will happen again in my career. Elsewhere it wouldn't have attracted much attention, but everything that goes on at Ibrox is highly publicised.

'In the short-term, I had to rise above the reject jibes. It had an adverse effect on my whole family. But we emerged stronger for the experience. The Rangers players were very supportive and helped a great deal, but it was a very trying time for all concerned.

'Obviously I wasn't in the manager's plan and I knew it was time to move on. I had a chance to join Charlton and other opportunities were under consideration when Alex Totten called me one morning with the invitation to Perth.

'I knew he had tried to sign me twice before. I asked him for the weekend to think about my future and, after talking things through with my wife Elizabeth, I opted for St Johnstone.'

Secrets, in football, are few and far between. The game thrives on gossip and the grapevine, idle talk and tittle-tattle. But Saints kept their next appointment cloaked in a veil of secrecy worthy of the KGB and, on May 25, they announced the latest addition to Scottish soccer's United Nations colony.

Sergei Baltacha's curriculum vitae kept company with the very best: four league championship medals and a quartet of domestic cup successes with Dynamo Kiev; a European Cup Winners' Cup triumph; an Olympic bronze; forty seven full international honours, World Cup campaigns and a European Championship final joust with Dutch superstars Ruud Gullit and Marco Van Basten. Now, at 32, he was seeking soccer asylum in Scotland, with St Johnstone. The obvious question was: Why?

'I must admit I'd never heard of the club until my good friend Ian Redford mentioned they might be interested when my contract at Ipswich was ending. He got things going and I travelled to Perth with my family to meet the manager and chairman,' explained Sergei, a player drawn from a different league than any other in St Johnstone's history and the first Soviet to earn a living in Scottish football. 'I felt the club had a future but I wanted assurances that I would be played as a sweeper.

'As a child of 12 or 13 I attended a special sports school. I represented my republic and the national under 16 side as a striker but ever since turning professional with Dynamo Kiev at 18 I played as a sweeper. If I wasn't being offered that role there was no chance of moving to Scotland. I still enjoy playing football, but only in the role I understand.'

A consummate professional contemplating a coaching career, Baltacha maintains habits fostered in his youth at sports retreats favoured by the famous Kiev club. Most afternoons, he enjoys a short nap and his diet is heavy on fresh fruit. Scottish fried fare is shunned and once, when the team tackled fish suppers after a midweek match, the Ukrainian refused to be tempted as his team-mates tucked in with relish.

'It's important I watch what I eat, especially at my age, and rest is vital to an athlete. Maybe Soviet players think more about these things than the Scots. But then it's a harder life in my homeland. Football meant I could provide for my family.'

With only two remaining places in Scotland for non-EEC footballers, Saints recruited local MP Sir Nicholas Fairbairn to lobby their case for a work permit at the Scottish Office. With no chance of reserving a place for Baltacha, it was essential to navigate the the diplomatic channels in haste.

'There was a communications problem with Dynamo Kiev to contend with. In addition to the language problems, we discovered that the Soviet club was closing down for the duration of the World Cup. It supplied the bulk of the international squad and even the office staff were taking a holiday or heading for Italy,' explained Geoff Brown.

'We had only 48 hours to hammer out the contract with the Soviets, involving on-going monthly payments, otherwise we might have missed the boat. By the time Kiev officials returned from Italy, the work permits in Scotland might have been snapped up. It was certainly a tighter timetable than we would have liked. But we were delighted when the deal came together.'

Strong arm tactics from John Inglis.

Closer to home, Saints enticed the rapidly maturing talents of 23-year-old John Inglis from Meadowbank to dovetail with Baltacha as the bedrock of the Perth defence. Having outlined his shopping list to the chairman, the manager returned from a welcome Spanish family holiday to find the deal signed and sealed. At £115,000, it meant another record fee for the Perth club.

One of the few stars to escape Jim McLean's firmament at Tannadice, Inglis served his apprenticeship with East Fife and Brechin before the third club in the capital's pecking order provided hometown football. Reputedly the paciest player in the First Divsion, Meadowbank Stadium might have suited him better had he pursued a track and field career. As it was, only rarely was the atmosphere conducive to soccer.

With Hearts and English clubs like Charlton and Stoke hovering, Saints moved in decisively. Totten, who had been frustrated in a bid to bring Inglis to Perth from Brechin, knew his chairman had concluded a bit of sharp business in his absence. This, he believed, was a future Scotland international in the making.

An ambitious individual with concrete career plans, Inglis was sold on the move to Perth by three principal factors: the stadium, the manager and the Premier shop window. He admitted to a degree of apprehension but saw it as the next stage in an ongoing learning process.

'Alex Totten had always impressed me with his drive and his ambition. I knew I was going to a club that was looking towards future development and that was important to me. Not everyone shared that opinion before the start of the season, but it was apparent to me that they would have to be taken seriously.

'I've always set myself goals in life and I'm never happy until I've achieved them. I'm prepared to work hard at my game and learn, in the hope I can go on to bigger things. For instance, the English First Division has always appealed to me. I think it would suit my style of play. I'm not in a great hurry, but this is a short career and you've got to make the most of it.'

With an eye to the future, 23-year-old Iain Lee was bought in a package which saw £20,000 and Mike Smith leave McDiarmid. There were inquiries further down the line for other personnel, including a bid to bring far-travelled Ian Redford back to his Perthshire roots, an offer for Dundee's Ian Angus (losing out to Motherwell) and a knock-back at Newcastle for one Paul Sweeney.

The Geordie side, in fact, featured in the warm-up programme mapped out by the Perth management, winning 3-1 at McDiarmid. Earlier, Saints had lingered in the north of England for five days, working out against Darlington and Rotherham. The Durham University campus provided the backdrop for a learning process designed to familiarise the players with each other and offer a crash course in Premier League survival techniques.

The trawl through the First Division was stepped up apace and, on the eve of the Premier opener, Morton accepted £100,000 for midfield combatant Tommy Turner. The 26-year-old toasted full-time football and departure from labours in the Chivas Regal whisky bond in Paisley.

Other managers had been impressed with the array of talents at Turner's disposal, but they ran scared of a glaring disciplinary flaw. Totten remarked: 'Turner always impressed me when we played against Morton, including our Scottish Cup matches. He was always involved in the action at the top level. Other managers weren't willing to take a chance with Tommy.'

Turner had grafted in the Premier arena twice before, with Morton occupying the bottom rung in 1984/85, while Saints were sinking into Division Two, and again in 1987/88. Both campaigns saw the Greenock club hit the century mark in the goals against column.

'I'd been with Morton for seven seasons and while I had supported them as a youngster, full-time football was what I really wanted. I'd always hoped to earn a living out of the game but I was prepared for yet another season at Greenock. In fact, I'd played against Motherwell in a Skol Cup defeat before manager Allan McGraw contacted the work to say Alex Totten wanted to talk terms,' said Turner.

'We met in a Paisley hotel but even before that I knew I would sign. I desperately wanted the move to full-time football in the Premier League. I'd got fed up with people saying this team and that team were interested in signing me and nothing further happening. But this one was for real and I wasn't going to knock it back.

'I reckon a lot of my disciplinary problems stemmed from sheer frustration. I always wanted to win — and that didn't happen too often when Morton were in the Premier League. We got some right hammerings. On one occasion, we lost 7-1 to Dundee United, with Paul Sturrock hitting five.'

Several of his new colleagues confessed Turner would not have featured highly in a straw poll designed to measure the popularity of opponents. But the player himself took that as a compliment to his on-field presence: 'My style doesn't always appeal to the opposition. But now I know if I'm getting kicked up and down the park it's because the other team are trying to stop me playing. I can handle the hard stuff and now I like to think I can handle the wind-ups as well.'

With Turner on the payroll, Totten mapped out his ambitions for the Premier campaign: 'I wanted the fans to be realistic about our prospects. Obviously I had experienced this level of football with Rangers, but few of the players knew what they were facing. The impact of Graeme Souness had brought better players to Scotland and it was a tougher arena than ever.

'I knew that our primary goal had to be avoiding relegation. When I said we would be delighted to finish in ninth place I was perfectly serious. This was shaping up to be one of the most crucial seasons in the history of the club. Survival was the name of the game.'

Confounding the Critics

IN an earlier decade, that doyen of sports writers, Hugh McIlvanney, celebrated the achievement of Alex Ferguson and a Saints side on the up escalator in Paisley.

Ferguson, later to guide Aberdeen to that famous European Cup Winners' Cup triumph, before opting for Old Trafford and carbon copy success, simply transformed Love Street. Marvelling at miracles wrought by Ferguson at St Mirren, McIlvanney reflected: 'As a case of revitalisation it lost out to Lazarus, but only in a photo-finish.'

Yet St Johnstone's impact on the Premier League surely projects another name into the frame. Nearly four years to the day that Alex Totten strolled out onto Muirton Park for the traditional photo-call accompanying any managerial appointment, he strode onto an altogether different stage: at Glasgow's plush Grosvenor Hotel, to accept the generous applause of 300 guests and Scotland's Manager of the Year award, sponsored by Scottish Brewers.

A team that ought to have been languishing on the lower rung of the ladder had carved out a respectable niche, with Perth fans still harbouring hopes of autumnal excursions to the continent as season 1990/91 entered April month. It was ample testimony to the daunting commitment given by many to the club over a five-year period.

Even a frustrating turn-of-the-year form slump couldn't mask the respect commanded by St Johnstone in securing an elevation in the Scottish game unprecedented for 20 years. Not since Willie Ormond introduced the Perthshire public to their one and only taste of European football had Saints been on such a high.

Plush McDiarmid welcomed crowds averaging around 7,700,

satellite receivers across Europe received soccer from Perth and the club's first Scottish Cup final had been but 90 minutes away. Could this really be the same club that hovered on the brink of extinction just five years earlier?

Since Totten's appointment the fans had enjoyed promotion, a replayed Scottish Cup semi-final with Rangers and the First Division championship. But this had been 12 months to top them all.

En route to the First Division championship, St Johnstone refused to have their early season programme cluttered by Skol Cup intrusions. While defeat at Dumfries ensured earnings from this particular tournament fell into the small beer bracket, the players could focus their attention and channel their energies into the serious task of promotion.

The strategy had served Saints well, but with an inexperienced Clyde team asked to visit Perth, expectant fans assumed a straightforward passage to the next phase of the 1990 competition.

But the itinerant Glasgow club, renting accommodation from Partick Thistle and later victims of relegation, inflicted a sorely embarrassing two-goal defeat, courtesy of spirited resistance and suicidal defensive blunders which suggested St Johnstone's interest in the Premier League would be brief and far from painless.

The Perth management had four days to cure the ills which afflicted a team in its entirety before Dundee United came to town for the first Tayside derby of the season. In the inaugural season of the Premier Division, back in 1975, the Tannadice club also guested in the opening league fixture and little more than 3,000 fans parted with their money at the Muirton turnstiles.

As an indication of St Johnstone's progress, police demanded the August 1990 engagement have all-ticket status. It seemed sensible enough, given that this was McDiarmid Park's offical introduction to the big time and opposition from the other end of the Carse of Gowrie provided an attractive bill. With the championship flag to be unfurled and the weather welcoming, a full house was anticipated.

Surprisingly, there were 2,385 vacant seats at the matinee and the missing fans had reasons aplenty to regret their decision to

Mark Treanor continues the downfall of the Dons.

give the curtain raiser a miss. Saints lost out 3-1 in a pulsating drama and found that all-action enthusiasm would have to be tempered with a measure of caution to prolong the stay at this level.

Midfielder Harry Curran signalled notice of exploits to come with a first-half goal, levelling a dubious Darren Jackson penalty. But the United striker, himself en route to heady heights in the scoring charts, pounced again before the interval.

With the early departure of United keeper Alan Main — the first victim of a pre-season edict aimed at stamping out the so-called professional foul — Saints had 35 minutes to ease past stand-in custodian Dave Bowman. Instead, amidst a flurry of corner kicks, United dumped the Perth side with a classic counter punch, via teenage prodigy Christian Dailly. If Alex Totten's pupils were to emerge with credit in this company, it was clear they would have to learn, and quickly.

A share of the spoils at Paisley eased Saints and their cautious 5-3-2 line-up onto the boards but Motherwell, one of the sides pinpointed as a stepping stone to safety, inflicted a three goal thrashing at Fir Park. It proved to be a defeat of immense significance.

Said Totten: 'John Balavage was ruled out through illness and Steve Maskrey sustained a facial wound minutes into the match. As it transpired team doctor Alistair McCracken was a familiar face around the ground. It was probably our most comprehensive defeat of the season and, without Lindsay Hamilton — making his debut — the score would have been much worse.'

That prompted a less brittle defensive strategy based on tight man to man marking, with Sergei Baltacha revelling in the sweeper role. It heralded a timely return to the fluent attacking style which had brought success in the past and proved that talk of sinking ships, even among the players, was premature.

The visit of Dunfermline introduced Hamilton to the Perth crowd. Naturally he had been hoping the number one jersey would be his from the outset but he respected the manager's loyalty to John Balavage.

'That home debut was the most nerve-wracking match of my life,' confessed the newcomer. 'I'd played half a game against Newcastle, but this was the real thing. I'd had a good pre-season but it was hard taking over from someone like John, who had been such a good friend to the club. He was a difficult act to follow.

'I'm a self-confident person by nature, but I admit I felt ill before the kick-off. And I didn't feel too clever when I lost a goal to Istvan Kozma in only seven minutes. It wasn't the best of starts in front of the home crowd. On reflection, we won the match 3-2 to clock up our first win, but on a personal note I felt my performance wasn't up to the standard I demand.'

That injury consigned Balavage, a £10,000 1984 signing from Albion Rovers, to a diet of reserve team football for the rest of the season: 'I was thrilled when the manager gave me the chance to hold onto my place at the start of the season and I'd been hoping to maintain my position a wee bit longer. But full credit to Lindsay, he took his chance and turned in some superb performances.

'I'd known for some time that my days were numbered, simply because the manager was going to prefer the full-time players. As the season progressed, it got to the stage that I hadn't even met the newer recruits. That's simply the way it is when you're not part of the main set-up — and that had been my choice.'

After a frustrating single goal defeat at Easter Road, Saints had notched up three points from 10: a considerable improvement on their previous foray into the top flight when seven games passed without anything tangible to show for their sweat and toil. Along the way, 24 goals were conceded.

On that occasion, the computer had been cruel in composing

'Gimme Five!' Steve Maskrey and Tommy Turner celebrate the defeat of the Dons.

the fixtures list. This time, it had been more kindly. But the programme took on a daunting look, with successive matches looming against the five teams reckoned to enjoy elite status in Scotland. The Old Firm, the New Firm and Hearts were held to be immune from the ills of relegation. St Johnstone were still being diagnosed as the most likely casualty come May and the next few weeks looked set to see the most grievous of wounds inflicted.

But on September 29, St Johnstone Football Club recorded the most astonishing pick-me-up-and-dust-me-down result in their century-plus history and, in so doing, earned their Premier spurs. Come 4.42 p.m. precisely, the Famous Grouse electronic scoreboard read, incredibly: St Johnstone 5, Aberdeen 0. Had the operator been a dash liberal with the sponsor's product?

Certainly, the result provoked consternation, and check-up calls, from sports desks around the country. Had some weary copytaker's fingers lapsed into a frightful fankle? On the results teleprinter, it warranted letters spelling out the margin of victory.

Aberdeen, a team of international renown brimming with players experienced in the ways of Scottish and Dutch representative squads, had lost their grip on the Skol Cup by a single semi-final goal to Rangers. But the McDiarmid visit was seen as a mere formality en route to recovery. The last occasion Saints scored against the Dons could be traced back to 1975 and a Jim O'Rourke goal. This fixture was viewed as a cast-iron certainty for fixed odds followers contemplating the weekend aways.

'Before the match, I recall asking the players to believe in themselves as a team. They had the ability to make their mark in the Premier League, but only if they could muster more self-belief. They responded and how!' said the manager. 'That was the launchpad for our season. It was a special day, never to be forgotten, in the history of this club.'

The scoreline, as one would expect, was economical with the truth. The gulf between the two sides should have been more extensive! Observers agreed that eight, even nine, would not have flattered the super Saints that afternoon.

Aberdeen were reduced to 10 men with the dismissal of full-back David Robertson around the half-hour mark. By that time Roddy Grant had inflicted the start of the damage and a Mark Treanor double extended the advantage to three before the interval. Grant and Maskrey encouraged the bewildered visiting fans to vacate the premises early for the miserable homeward journey.

In the Granite City, the *Press and Journal* conducted a front page post mortem into the locals' heftiest defeat since 1969. 'Dons fans lament their team's humiliation' blared the headline, suitably bordered in black. The sports pages displayed more sensitivity for the feelings of those involved: 'Bizarre goings on at Perth'.

Respected journalist and club biographer, Jack Webster, admitted: 'I cannot recall a clear 5-0 scoreline in 48 years of following the Dons. It is the most astonishing result I can remember. It defies analysis. It is exasperating, but it is one of those extraordinary one-off things.'

Seven years previously, Aberdeen had doled out a five goal

Heartbreaker: Tommy Turner scores at Tynecastle.

hiding to St Johnstone on Premier business, with men like Joe Miller (twice), Eric Black, Mark McGhee and Billy Stark to the fore. Later that season, John Hewitt, with a hat trick, Gordon Strachan and Peter Weir repeated the punishment. Results like that made the taste of revenge all the sweeter for delirious Perth fans in the 8,711 crowd.

Toasting his fourth anniversary as chairman, Geoff Brown admitted: 'I can't remember us scoring a goal against Aberdeen, let alone five. What I found very hard to believe was that Aberdeen never really came at us. They seemed to be playing for time to avoid conceding another goal.'

Displaying admirable dignity in defeat, stunned Aberdeen boss Alex Smith confessed the entire 90 minutes had been 'a total nightmare'. By Monday morning, he had recovered sufficiently to announce: 'On behalf of the team, our sincere apologies.'

It may have been mere co-incidence, but with Perth on an unprecedented soccer high, the district was hailed as the Best of British in an academic quality of life survey. But now the Premier shock troops faced an invitation to visit the East End of the European City of Culture. Could they turn on the exhibition stuff in such a hostile environment?

If Lindsay Hamilton had been disappointed with his McDiarmid debut performance, the reviews were ecstatic at Celtic Park. Before 27,000 fans, the third biggest crowd in Britain that day, the man branded a Rangers reject by the Press turned in an immaculate display as Saints fashioned a scoreless draw.

One late reflex save, from the head of Celtic starlet Gerry Creaney, helped Saints and Hamilton make their point. The keeper revealed that one-time Parkhead idol Ronnie Simpson had been recruited by Alex Totten to develop his game.

'Being the only full-time keeper at the club posed problems and the manager invited Ronnie along to coach me once a week. He proved a great help in an advisory capacity as the season unfolded,' said Hamilton. 'As a former international with a European Cup medal to his name, he's a man to respect. I also found he wasn't in it for any personal glory, he simply wanted to help improve my game.'

In another imaginative move, Totten recruited 71-year-old Glaswegian sprint coach Jimmy Campbell to pep up the pace of the players. The former dentist pulled out all the stops to mould the Perth squad into Toughs of the Track. Full-time football made that kind of initiative possible.

Saints felt they were entitled to both points from the Parkhead trip, with Allan Moore blatantly downed by Ireland World Cup hero Pat Bonner just minutes before the break. But Celtic, minus midfield captain Paul McStay, might have quibbled justifiably had they lost out on a point. Mark Treanor, a two-goal hero in the demolition of the Dons, maintained the Parkhead performance provided greater satisfaction: 'The Press and the fans were saying the Aberdeen win was a one-off, so that was a thoroughly professional effort in Glasgow.'

Certainly the manager was quick to highlight the all-round quality of the team and, crucially, he underlined the importance of continuity in the selection process. En route to the Tartan Special Manager of the Month award for October, Totten's team was picking itself, threading together seven consecutive matches with the starting line-up unchanged.

'Maybe I had been too cautious at the start of the campaign,' said the manager. 'We couldn't throw caution to the wind and we didn't want to give away goals. Other newcomers to the Premier League were not averse to stringing five men across the back and hoping for a break at the other end.

'After the Motherwell defeat, we decided to ring the changes, reverting to tactics which gave free rein to our three attackers. It had brought us promotion but I had feared the possible consequences of introducing it in the top division. As it turned out, the system suited the players and it seemed to catch teams off-guard in the early months.'

Next up were Hearts, with recently installed manager Joe Jordan at the helm and European victory over Soviet side Dnepr boosting morale down the Gorgie Road. For players like Allan Moore and Paul Cherry, this was familiar territory. Roddy Grant, on the other hand, was better acquainted with the Tynecastle terracing than the field of play — but there was no question of divided loyalties, as he proved with a dazzling second goal and two assists.

Hearts had finished joint runners-up to Rangers the previous season but Saints had warned already they were no respecters of reputations. Grant plagued international defensive duo Dave McPherson and Craig Levein all afternoon to earn the man of the match accolade, but he was ably supported by Sergei Baltacha, John Inglis and a host of others.

Saints lost their Tommy Turner lead in the most controversial of circumstances. A corner kick returning to play introduced a linesman to Sergei Baltacha and his ever-improving command of the English language. The spirit of free speech may have been abroad in Baltacha's homeland, but glasnost remains a touch radical for Scotland's sensitive football hierarchy. It merited a booking, but answered any lingering doubts about his communication skills on the park!

Inglis acknowledged: 'Without a player of Sergei's experience in defence, my introduction to the Premier League might have been more daunting. We talk about football on and off the park and he's taught me so much about the game, fitness and diet. Our styles complement each other and it's certainly good for my confidence knowing he's at the back.

'The Hearts match was one to remember for me because, had things worked out differently, I might have been playing for them. Coming from the Edinburgh area, I knew many of the players and marking a proven goalscorer like John Robertson was quite a challenge. But throughout the season, I learned that none of the Scottish strikers relished close man-marking — in fact some of them lost interest if they were denied space.

'With previous clubs I'd played zonal defence and man-marking is physically demanding. But I'd like to think fitness is one of my biggest assets and at that stage of the season we were playing well as a unit. We'd settled into a rhythm and the results were going our way.'

With the Tynecastle match again levelled, Harry Curran

ghosted into the danger zone 10 minutes from the end to slot home the winner. His intrusions from midfield were vital throughout the season, answering the challenge to support the strikers with remarkable success.

It was apparent Saints were reaping the benefit of Baltacha's immense experience, his timely tackling, composure and ability to transform defence into attack with a single well-directed pass. Already, he had forged a close understanding with defensive partner, Inglis, whose leech-like marking capabilities masked further invaluable talents tailored to the Premier arena.

With Paul Cherry and Mark Treanor, recalling two previous top flight campaigns with Clydebank, revelling in their minder chores, Saints looked secure at the back. In central midfield, anchorman Gary McGinnis provided the defensive foil for more adventurous excursions by Harry Curran, while the inexhaustible Tommy Turner was in fine fettle.

Up front, the pace and trickery of Allan Moore and Steve Maskrey was complemented by the hustle and bustle of centre forward Roddy Grant. All in all, it was a heady, potent brew which Saints fans relished and rivals found most unpalatable.

Never before had Saints survived four Premier matches undefeated, but with the Ibrox championship favourites making their acquaintance with McDiarmid Park, there was much talk of bubbles bursting in media circles. Was this where the upstarts got their comeuppance?

An intriguing contest was in prospect, not least because Baltacha would be matching-up against former Dynamo Kiev colleague Oleg Kuznetsov, playing his second match for the Ibrox club since a £1.4 million cheque had Graeme Souness assuring the faithful they had a player genuinely worthy of the world class accolade.

The clamour for tickets was such that Alex Totten alone was required to field more than 100 calls from friends and acquaintances, old and new, anxious to take in the game. It was no surprise that a new ground record, with 10,504 ticket holders occupying seats, was established on October 20. But with 10,721 available, there remained scope for improvement.

Naturally, Totten's Ibrox connection was cast up again in the pre-match hype. But on this occasion, Lindsay Hamilton and the

A couple of toppers: Alex Totten and Allan Moore.

Soviet angle deflected much of the media attention. The reject label went with the territory, but the keeper was determined to maintain an air of dignity in the build-up to the first match against his former club.

Baltacha was equally reticent to prompt controversy, refusing even a forecast for the hacks: 'It's a Russian tradition, a superstition, not to talk about the result before the match. It's unlucky.'

Perhaps his old chum Kuznetsov had hinted at the outcome, if only to family, interpreter or colleagues. For whatever reason, misfortune felled him after seven minutes, consigning him to a miserable haul back to full fitness via California, where specialists delicately reconstructed his career prospects.

The challenge, by Curran, was innocuous by any standards. The Soviet found his studs rooted to the spot before tumbling to the turf. It marked the end of the season for Oleg and a cooling of diplomatic relations between the two clubs.

The enforced departure of the Soviet sweeper posed problems for Rangers and they were grateful to escape Perth with a point. The scoreless draw was an undeniable moral victory for St Johnstone, taking their first Premier point from the Ibrox club. Not since 1970 had Rangers left the Fair City without a win bonus.

Lindsay Hamilton added a shut-out to file with the Aberdeen

and Celtic results, and spent much of the 90 minutes admiring the international capabilities of England's Chris Woods at the opposite end of the pitch.

Allan Moore was at his magnificent best, persecuting the revamped Rangers rearguard. He led his marker a merry dance and Rangers survived to the interval under siege. The corner kick count ran at two to one in favour of Saints, but when the dust finally settled on a full-blooded affair, honours were even . . . although the despondent faces of those bound for Glasgow suggested otherwise.

The match, ultimately remembered for an unsavoury aftermath, also provided one of the soccer season's most heartwarming stories, when young team mascot Frazer Waugh fulfilled a year-long dream by leading his St Johnstone heroes onto the field.

Twelve months earlier, the Crieff Primary pupil collapsed at the Manchester United glamour game to open McDiarmid Park. Only timely treatment by Perth staff and local ambulancemen gave hospital medics a chance to save Frazer's life.

He survived a critical brain haemorrhage, two cardiac arrests and complex surgery. The family paid warm tribute to the influence of manager Alex Totten and then club captain Don McVicar for bedside visits. A promise was made that, if Saints reached the Premier League, Frazer could lead out the Perth team against Rangers. It was a promise everyone connected with the club was delighted to fulfil.

On the match itself, Alex Totten insisted: 'My players proved to the country that their recent results were thoroughly deserved.' Ominously, Graeme Souness was to remark, somewhat ruefully: 'Welcome to Scotland, Oleg.' His powder was kept dry for a more dramatic verbal volley to come.

It was all too hurry-scurry for the purist, and the Ibrox management: 'We were happy with a point. Saints were aggressive . . . very aggressive. But they played with fire and determination and deserved a lot of credit for that.'

All pretty placid, really. The lull before the storm, it transpired. Several days later, with Rangers on a daunting European Cup expedition to Belgrade, Souness launched a barely disguised attack on St Johnstone and, by implication, Harry Curran.

Bemoaning the loss of Kuznetsov, Souness maintained: 'It's too tough in Scotland. We sign players because of their skill, not as hammer throwers.'

While every club has a player who floats like a battleship and stings like a B52, Curran, at 5 feet 9 inches tall and short of 12 stone, cut an unlikely figure to be labelled 'Dirty Harry'. On those rare occasions his name is sought, it's the lash of the tongue rather than the tackling which has incurred the wrath of the referee.

'Those remarks were laughable, total nonsense,' he maintained. 'How many times do players bump into each other in the course of a game? I know in my own mind I did nothing to harm Kuznetsov and fortunately the television cameras were there to prove it.

'I came in for a bit of ribbing from the guys about being a hammer thrower but that was a laugh. They know it's not my style. In fact, the boss is forever saying I should be getting in more tackles.'

Baltacha, who partnered Kuznetsov for many years in the Kiev defence, requested permission to see his friend in the dressing room after the game: 'Of course I felt sorry for Oleg but he said that there was no problem with the tackle. He twisted his knee when he fell. When you have to play important matches for club and country, including the World Cup that summer, there is little chance for rest. That did not help Oleg.

'Graeme Souness is an emotional man and he had spent a lot of money to get the best defender in the Premier League. The manager was upset at losing the player. But Oleg himself said Harry was not to blame.'

While the folks back home came to terms with the Belgrade bombshell, the *Rangers News* took Totten to task, accusing their former employee of sour grapes and of mounting 'a bitter attack' on the Ibrox club.

Totten refused to be drawn, simply stating: 'They took my comments the wrong way entirely. In comparing my team, which had cost £500,000, with the multi-million-pound international players of Rangers, I was trying to emphasise just how well we had performed. We annihilated them that day. Chris Woods was in peak form, while Lindsay Hamilton had to make only one real save.'

The Rangers match signalled the quarter mark in a compelling season for Perth fans. The nine points obtained exceeded the wildest estimations of the critics and provided the perfect platform for consolidation. Ironically, Saints most productive assignments had been against more fancied opposition.

Having measured themselves against the best Scottish football had to offer, it was a battle-hardened and street-wise side which prepared for the return engagement with table-topping Dundee United. Jim McLean's side led the field, undefeated, and retained an interest in the UEFA Cup, but their form rating didn't impress Perth captain Gary McGinnis.

Having taken over the armband from Don McVicar, temporarily eased out of the picture after the Motherwell defeat, McGinnis ventured the opinion that United weren't performing to the level their results sequence might suggest. He commented: 'They've been picking up points but someone is due to give them a beating — why not us?'

Bold words, indeed. Reckless even, given that statisticians dusting down the records books discovered the corresponding fixture some seven years before resulted in a record Premier hiding for the Fair City travelling fraternity. Paul Hegarty, Richard Gough, Billy Kirkwood and doubles from Eamonn Bannon and Davie Dodds ensured journalists found their command of arithmetic put to the test.

But Saints made the short trip to the City of Discovery in adventurous mood, confidence steeled by six points from eight at the expense of the country's other top clubs. It proved to be one of the most complete and thoroughly professional performances of the year.

Twelve minutes from the end, Darren Jackson reduced St Johnstone's well-earned two-goal advantage. Up to that point, the Perth side had dominated the match with consummate ease, to the patent delight of a particularly vociferous support. Alex Totten recalled: 'Our fans were singing "There's Only One Team in Tayside" that afternoon. I rather liked that!'

With Scotland national coach Andy Roxburgh settled in the stand, Saints eased ahead through John Inglis — already the most highly rated asset on the Perth payroll — with his sole strike of the season. Another from Steve Maskrey before the interval proved

Me and my shadow: Roddy Grant tussles with Paul Elliott.

crucial. Tommy Turner, playing his last match before a four-week suspension, was simply immense as Saints secured fourth place, only three points off the pace.

Inglis, whose teenage world caved in when United decided it was time to part company before his 17th birthday, took particular pleasure from the result: 'My mother was in the stand to see me for the first time in senior football so that goal made it extra special. Even by that stage I felt I'd come to terms with the demands of the Premier League. I wondered what was in store for us after the first few games, but for a side with so many new faces we knitted together quickly.'

Defeat at home to St Mirren and a Sigmunder Torfason goal followed, leaving the manager of the month flatter than the dregs of last night's pint. Even B and Q Skills winner Allan Moore couldn't provide the necessary inspiration.

The build-up to the Hibs match was overshadowed by moves designed to bring veteran Belgian World Cup captain Frankie Vercauteren to Perth. With 12 years at Anderlecht and three at Nantes, where he forged a friendship with Maurice Johnston and agent Bill McMurdo, Saints noted an interest in recruiting the left-sided midfielder.

A significant bid lodged for Paul Sweeney was blocked and there was further disappointment for Saints when the Vercauteren deal was strangled by bureaucratic red tape and financial rowing on the continent. Any further moves to recruit ageing internationals eager to supplement their retirement fund in Scotland were left to others.

Instead, Saints dipped into the First Division to entice stylish 24-year-old John Davies from Clydebank, with the £165,000 cheque breaking new ground for the Perth board. Totten noted: 'I remembered John from my time at Ibrox, when he was a teenager. He was a cultured footballer and like Mark Treanor he experienced the Premier League with Clydebank. He also had a spell with Swedish side Jonkoping. It was vital to boost our squad as the season progressed and, like so many other ambitious young players, I knew he would benefit from our full-time set-up.'

A share of the spoils with cash-starved Hibernian preceded the precarious journey north to Aberdeen. Manager Alex Smith, secure in the knowledge that wins over Hearts, Celtic and St Mirren had the championship challenge ticking over, insisted: 'We're not going to be caught up in any infantile revenge stuff.'

But he reckoned without an intrusion by a firm of North East solicitors with a flair for publicity. A bounty of £5,000 was offered to the Dons if they could avenge the five goal defeat at the first time of asking.

But Aberdeen, protecting an undefeated home record stretching back to Boxing Day, found playmaker Jim Bett smothered by McGinnis, while Inglis and Cherry snuffed out the forward threat posed by Dutch international Hans Gillhaus and emerging home-grown talent Eoin Jess. Keeper Lindsay Hamilton departed with his fourth shut-out of the season, obtained against Aberdeen and the Old Firm. The reward, on offer for three seasons, was put on hold.

Saints made for East End Park with skipper McGinnis and Mark Treanor joining Turner in the sin bin. New man Davies, after a three-minute appearance at Pittodrie, enjoyed a starting place and part-timer Doug Barron featured in the back four as the first double scalp was taken.

Harry 'The Hit Man' Curran.

'There weren't many first-team starts for the part-timers. We were only called upon in an emergency,' said Barron. 'For the first time in my career, I rarely had a match to play on a Saturday and it was difficult maintaining an appetite for the game.'

Another two points were bagged with victory over Motherwell before Ibrox, and the new championship pace-setters beckoned. On the bench for Saints was surprise £55,000 purchase Kenny MacDonald, after a two-minute outing the previous week. Eight years before, a previous regime had liberated the self-same player on a free transfer, before he proceeded to make an impact with Forfar, Airdrie and latterly Raith Rovers.

MacDonald's strike rate over the previous four seasons totalled more than 70. The management underlined that competition for places was vital for the club to maintain its momentum in the league and MacDonald offered cover for leader of the line Roddy Grant. However, the striker was transfer listed in May with Kenny Ward, Iain Lee and part-timers Doug Barron, Ian Heddle and John Balavage.

Saints went west knowing that potentially hazardous outings to Parkhead, Tynecastle, Tannadice, Pittodrie and East End Park had been surmounted without a sombre homeward journey. But Ibrox was a different matter altogether.

The scribes responsible for recording the last Saints victory in Govan weren't using papyrus, but it was nearly 20 years since that dynamic duo John Connolly and Henry Hall, on April 17, 1971, purloined the points en route to third place in the final tabulation. Saints and their bold run of one defeat in 10 outings didn't impress the bookies . . . or Rangers.

More than 34,000 customers braved the bite of deep mid-winter and most departed beaming broadly, having warmed to the dominance reflected in a 4-1 scoreline. Only a well-executed Roddy Grant turn and finish provided consolation as a fired-up Ibrox side exacted retribution for their considerable discomfort at Perth.

Mark Walters at his most tantalising on the wing couldn't be contained. Marker Paul Cherry, struggling with a tendon injury which was to demand an operation and force a premature end to his season admitted: 'Things were bad enough but I pulled a calf muscle early on. Walters was on form and he ripped me apart. Even if I'd been 100 per cent it would have been hard going — but I had no chance carrying an injury.'

Keeper Lindsay Hamilton, at that stage still involved in evening coaching sessions for Rangers youths, had hoped for happier circumstances for his Ibrox Premier debut. The Gers attack had been shut out at Perth but was psyched up for vengeance on home turf.

'Obviously the score was disappointing but what hurt more was the reaction of the Ibrox fans I'd always wanted to play in front of with Rangers. We didn't perform well and didn't deserve anything from the game but the abuse was over the top. My father was in the stand and the taunts hurt enormously.'

The bandwagon got rolling again with Davies (his first for Saints) and Maskrey edging out Hearts. Arguably the finest year in St Johnstone history entered the record books with one of the most memorable matches McDiarmid Park will ever host.

In a classic encounter, Celtic found their first visit to the stadium pointless. After striking with two goals from Maskrey and

New kids on the block: Kenny MacDonald, Paul Sweeney and John Davies —
and a £300,000 price tag.

Curran within the first six minutes, Turner added the all-important winner in a 3-2 victory to treasure.

'That must rank as one of our best team performances of the season, along with the win over United at Tannadice,' said Gary McGinnis, who in the passing noted that he had been Billy McNeill's first signing at Celtic Park. 'Mind you, Davie Provan was the first one Billy knew about. I was just a youngster and Sean Fallon handled all the details.'

In their lofty fourth place perch at the half-way phase of the Premier campaign, the Perth club had banked 21 points, to gain a five-point advantage on the Parkhead side. With an eight-point cushion from the relegation trapdoor, Father Christmas had called early at McDiarmid Park. As it transpired, a carbon copy of the points total would have ensured third place come May.

'What a fantastic year it had been for the club,' said Alex Totten, reflecting on a championship and an impact un-precedented at this level. 'St Johnstone was the name on everyone's lips and we were serving up entertaining football. After that match, an older Parkhead fan said our play reminded him of the old-fashioned Celtic style. That was a tremendous compliment.

'It's 12 months the fans will never forget and the team commanded respect from the best because of their whirlwind introduction to the top division. As a manager there's always pressure but it's marvellous when the team is winning. I read an article in which Alex MacDonald said that from Monday to Friday a manger's job is superb. It's the other bit that can be a problem. But thankfully that year the problems were minimal.'

The lucky white heather gifted for the opening of McDiarmid Park remained in place behind the managerial desk and the left sock was tucked into the shoe first, as Totten's routine demanded. The New Year, however, got off on the wrong foot, with Tommy Turner warranting the only Perth dismissal of the season — although a hefty 60 team bookings ensured the yellow card was flourished most weeks. Turner's indiscretion was compounded by a Ross Jack winner three minutes from the end and had the manager fuming: 'Turner let himself and his colleagues down. It was a crazy retaliation and it cost us dearly. He was fined heavily by the club.'

The following week, it was Saints' turn to leave it late, with only 60 seconds on the clock when close season injury victim Kenny Ward ensured a 2-2 result at Motherwell. But the elements intervened in the next few weeks to interrupt the rhythm of the Saints and action was confined to a semi-final spot in the annual Tennents Sixes.

The club remained in the headlines and the consistency of John Inglis prompted transfer conjecture in the tabloids. The player himself let it pass: 'Transfer talk affected my game the previous season with Meadowbank but this time I was better prepared to handle it. It was disappointing when the speculation didn't amount to anything but it wasn't unsettling. I knew within myself that I could improve areas of my game.'

Back to the real thing after the indoors diversion and a single goal at Paisley extended the points gap to confirm that whoever might be going down, it certainly wasn't going to be St Johnstone. It was no coincidence that before January was out, the spectre of relegation was vanquished from the Premier League, exorcised by a Scottish League reconstruction vote for Leagues of 12, 12 and 14.

Jockeying for position: Allan Moore is in the saddle.

St Johnstone, now classed among Scotland's Big Six, resented a rule change in mid-season. Chairman Geoff Brown explained: 'We started the season with each and every club knowing the score. We favoured extending the division, but only at the end of the season. Had St Johnstone been occupying the bottom berth, as had been expected, I doubt if the reconstruction proposals would have stood a cat in hell's chance of getting approval.'

The four clubs in most danger of dismissal — St Mirren, Hibs, Motherwell and Dunfermline — naturally sought self-preservation and hailed the Falkirk proposition as a beleaguered wagon train might once have welcomed the cavalry charging over the brow of the hill.

Said Totten: 'That decision made an absolute nonsense of the Scottish game and had a crucial effect on the way certain teams approached matches. It didn't help St Johnstone one iota and, in fact, it meant my players didn't get the enormous credit they deserved for what had been achieved. Had it been us in danger of dropping out of the Top Ten, reconstruction would have been a non-starter. The other teams would have bid us goodbye without a second thought.'

At one fell swoop, players conditioned to think in terms of avoiding relegation were being invited to raise their sights and focus on Europe. In the previous few weeks, Totten and Paton had been at pains to remind players of their priorities. Now, it was a whole new ball game.

Captain Gary McGinnis explained: 'I thought that decision was absolute lunacy, coming in the middle of the season. Obviously it helped certain teams and, with the full-time sides in the First Division investing heavily to gain promotion, they were bound to favour the plan. But it did us no favours.

'By that time our performances were demanding respect from the opposition, but the shake-up definitely undermined our game. The urgency that had been there before Christmas was missing in some of the later matches. The achievement of staying in the league was cheapened.'

Scheduled dates with Dundee United, Rangers and Hearts all fell victim to the weather and only desperate measures ensured a midweek engagement with Aberdeen proceeded as planned. BSkyB satellite coverage and the small matter of a £60,000 cheque for the first live soccer transmission from Perth inspired frantic efforts to protect the pitch from the ravages of the Big Chill.

Countless tons of straw were spread across the turf as this serious pay day loomed large. Saints had already announced they planned to examine the pitch protection options before the start of the new 44-game Premier League and critics sniped it was not before time.

'Why hadn't the club thought of that when the new stadium was planned?' they demanded. The answer was simple: even had the cash been available — and it wasn't — where was the economic sense in frittering away more than £100,000 to protect lower league fixtures and the often spartan attendances they inspired? Patently, there were greater priorities. Come the end of the season, after weighing up the pros and cons, the club opted for plastic sheeting, rather than undersoil heating.

Two midweek home matches, against the New Firm, proved to be the axis on which the rest of the league season revolved for St Johnstone. Assistant boss Bertie Paton explained: 'We appreciated those were important hurdles. Aberdeen and Dundee United were second and third in the table and victories offered a serious tilt at a European place.

'I so much wanted us to catch those two. There wasn't a great chasm in class to bridge. We'd already proved that with earlier results and another four points would have given us an enormous lift for the rest of the season.'

Sadly for Saints, late goals in two largely turgid affairs dealt devastating blows to the prospect of continental excursions come the autumn. Teenager Scott Booth settled the satellite match three minutes from time and luckless Paul Cherry, making his last appearance before taking to the operating table, conceded an own goal with 13 minutes to play against United. For the first time, Saints had lost two games back to back.

Totten pointed out: 'The Aberdeen game was touch and go when Theo Snelders dived on the ball outside his penalty area, just as Steve Maskrey was set to score. By the time they scored, a striker had been substituted by a defender. They were settling for a point. It was hard to accept that result.'

Nonetheless Europe still beckoned for the Perth club. They jetted out for a three-day break on the Costa del Sol, underlining the huge transformation in the club's fortunes. It was a chance to relax, enjoy a few libations and foster team morale.

For Alex Totten, there was a welcome opportunity to team up again with friend and mentor Jock Wallace. Terry Butcher, the recently installed Coventry manager, was also enjoying a winter break in the company of his new side. With a former employer in common, lulls in the conversation were few and far between!

The United match saw stylish defender John Inglis injured as Saints troubled run continued, with frustrated fans noting that their team hadn't found the net at McDiarmid since the December 22 win over Celtic. On February 26, Allan Moore ended the famine by calmly netting a breakaway goal against Rangers, later levelled by Dutchman Pieter Huistra.

If the previous McDiarmid battle of the blues had fanned the flames of controversy, this exchange set the back pages ablaze. Ibrox manager Graeme Souness, inviting yet another trek to SFA headquarters at Park Gardens, was livid as Rangers were relieved of their first point since December.

But comments questioning the standard of refereeing paled into insignificance as the Press feasted on further after match drama. A difference of opinion over the wellbeing of a kettle in the away dressing room engaged the Rangers manager/director in a frank exchange of views with Perth tea lady Aggie Moffat. Both parties were on the boil.

By the time chairman Geoff Brown called time-out, the Press had the makings of the 'Storm in a Tea Cup' story which brewed up nicely over the next few days. Rather than stir matters up further, St Johnstone declined to elaborate on this colourful controntation. But grateful cartoonists simply lapped it up.

A harsh three goal deficit at Parkhead saw Saints being pursued for fourth place by a Celtic side rejuvenated since the turn of the year and a 2-1 capital set-back brought Hearts into the hunt. The Tynecastle defeat ensured that Celtic eased ahead of the Perth side on goal difference with a match in hand. Psychologically, it was to prove a telling blow.

Further wheeling and dealing to bolster the squad culminated in a £100,000 expenditure which, at last, brought 25-year-old Paul Sweeney onto the McDiarmid roster. A naturally left-sided player capable of midfield and defensive chores, he had been tracked for months by Alex Totten. Before joining Newcastle United, Sweeney had made an impression with Raith Rovers.

Sweeney, later to require an achilles tendon operation, and his new colleagues were on the wrong end of a 4-1 hiding from Motherwell, as Tommy McLean's side enjoyed their first away win of the season. With veteran Davie Cooper displaying the talents which culminated in the sports reporters Player of the Year award, Saints nosedived to their heftiest McDiarmid defeat.

Ironically, keeper Lindsay Hamilton was rightly hailed as man of the match. Ever the perfectionist, he lamented the loss of four goals — none of which he could have prevented. But manager Totten again inquired if there was a better keeper in Scotland, with specialist coach Ronnie Simpson maintaining: 'Lindsay has come on a ton this season. I've given this a lot of thought and, quite honestly, he's now ready for international honours. He really is in that class.'

Even Hamilton's capabilities couldn't halt the Saints slide, however, and defeat at Dunfermline, followed by a creditable scoreless draw with Dundee United, meant that any realistic Perth prospects of hosting European competition for only the second time were focused on the Scottish Cup. The Tannadice match featured a shadow selection, with the regional rivals' next date assuming enormous significance.

Captain Gary McGinnis acknowledges the fans.

In the wake of reconstruction and a disappointing Premier sequence, Saints sought solace in the Tennents backed trophy. Berwick Rangers, 24 years on from THE cup shock, produced a sterling display to defy the Perth club and warrant a midweek replay south of the border.

More than 3,000 observers ensured one of Shielfield Park's healthier crowds in more than a decade and in a seven goal thriller, Saints hailed Allan Moore as their hero with an extra-time decider which set up a home tie with hapless Hibs.

Minus the services of Inglis and Cherry, Totten's selection struggled to contain the physical presence of target man Keith Houchen in an opening period which saw the Edinburgh side in command, and in the lead. But only minutes from the interval, the temperamental striker aimed a kick at Tommy Turner and played no further part in the proceedings. It proved fatal to the capital club's hopes of further financial in-put from the cup.

'That was the turning point,' said Totten. 'We were positive, bringing on Kenny Ward for defender Mark Treanor and Hibs were put under siege for the entire second half. They retreated into a defensive shell but Steve Maskrey and Roddy Grant produced the goods when it mattered. Roddy left it until the final minute. It might not have been good for the nerves, but it ruled out any comeback for the opposition.'

Once more the draw favoured Saints with a home tie. Ayr United, struggling in the lower reaches of the First Division, stood between Totten and his second Scottish Cup semi-final achievement in three years. Putting it in perspective, victory would hoist the Fair City side into the final four for only the fourth time in their 107-year history.

Former favourite Sammy Johnston, returning to the city on business for the first time since a £50,000 September transfer, wanted to win more than most, but first quarter goals from Roddy Grant and Steve Maskrey threatened disappointment. With Saints cruising, Ayr created a stir and two strikes suggested both teams would be asked to play it again in midweek. But that was to reckon without Allan Moore and another telling cup contribution.

With substitute Don McVicar supplying the ammunition, the diminutive winger vacated his touchline berth to fire an astonishing 10-minute hat-trick of headers: 'I'd scored one previous first-team hat-trick, the first at McDiarmid Park. This one was vital because we took our foot off the pedal and let Ayr back at us. The Press made a fuss because the goals were all headers, but I've got a good spring and try to get on the end of crosses.

'I scored nine all season and it could have been 19 if I'd taken my chances. I kept taking the wrong options when faced with a keeper. But I've never been a proven goalscorer and I was happy with my form at such a high level. I enjoy playing against Premier defenders, because their timing is better than First Division players and generally I don't take as much punishment.'

Moore's late intervention set up a Tayside semi-final derby for the right to meet Celtic or Motherwell at Hampden Park. The neutral venue selected for the Dundee United-St Johnstone clash was Dunfermline's East End Park, prompting disappointment for the personality player.

Moore complained: 'I had hoped it would be played at Hampden. It was my first semi-final and ever since turning professional I'd dreamed of playing in a match of this importance at the Mount Florida stadium. Dunfermline just didn't seem right, and the playing surface was a disgrace.'

Gary McGinnis, however, noted that while the open spaces of Hampden might have suited Saints style, the atmosphere would have suffered: 'East End was very compact which didn't suit our kind of football, but it was accessible for the fans of both teams.' The all-ticket crowd numbered 16,560.

Saints retreated to Dunblane Hydro for the pre-match countdown, well aware that the club's first ever Scottish Cup final place was but 90 minutes away. Unlike the semi-final joust with Rangers two years before, the Perth players appreciated this was a match that genuinely could be won. After all, they had taken three points from four against United at Tannadice.

'We knew we had a real chance of reaching the final. We weren't bragging or over confident but we knew it was within our capabilities,' said McGinnis, whose nine years under the McLean regime had included a semi-final substitute appearance. 'Living in Dundee, I was aware many United fans thought it would be a breeze for their team. But the players didn't see it that way.

'When Harry Curran equalised John Clark's opener before half-time I was convinced we could go on to win by a couple of goals. But we missed vital chances and mistakes cost us the tie. It wasn't a great game but even the more experienced United players confessed they carried the luck. How did we feel? Sick.'

Curran's headed equaliser contributed to an astonishing goals tally. The former double glazing installation expert was forever spotting windows of opportunity in opposition defences to top the Perth scoring charts with 11 goals. That proved an unrivalled strike rate from the Premier midfield and the rejuvenated Glaswegian found himself flanked by those whose season toils are judged by the goal standard.

Curran finished one ahead of Steve Maskrey and two in front of Roddy Grant and Allan Moore in the statistical chart adorning the manager's McDiarmid Park office wall.

'I set out with the aim of getting goals. The manager and Bertie Paton encouraged me to make runs into opposition penalty areas.

They felt that was my strength and, for much of the season, I had Gary McGinnis to thank for taking care of the defensive chores. Sometimes the fans don't appreciate Gary's qualities but he's a real player's player. His role isn't spectacular but it's essential for attack-minded team-mates like myself.'

With a meagre three goals to his name the previous season, Curran's form was a revelation for the Saints support. Modest enough to dismiss several as 'simple tap-ins', he was a vital component in Totten's tactics. His perpetual motion philosophy provided a vital element and assured automatic choice status.

For Lindsay Hamilton, who had celebrated the Ayr triumph with a spontaneous victory roll, it was the quickest match of his life: 'We didn't bottle it. They took their chances and we didn't. That was what it boiled down to in the end. I'd waited a long time to enjoy a run in the Scottish Cup and, like everyone at McDiarmid, I had hoped it would culminate in a final appearance.'

Sergei Baltacha, with more medals to his name than the average Red Army general, had relished the prospect of adding a Scottish Cup win to his roll of honour: 'That result was among the most disappointing of my career. I wanted a medal so badly and believed we could beat Dundee United.'

He continued: 'There are some great players in the Premier League. Ally McCoist is the man I rate the best striker. He has everything: pace, skill, a good brain and an instinct for goals. Other players to impress me were Mark Walters, Davie Cooper, Tommy Boyd and, in defence, Alex McLeish. But I would rate John Inglis as one of the top defenders in Scotland.

'It's not because he's a team-mate, I can assure you. At his age, he's one of the best I've seen. He has a big future and should play for Scotland. John is willing to learn and that's important, but he has speed and an excellent physical build. Very few players get the better of him.'

Baltacha attracted five bookings, the majority provoked by demonstrating an ever improving grasp of colloquial English to officialdom. But his wife, Olga, leapt to his defence: 'I understand Sergei's frustration with Scottish referees. I have watched him for 15 years and previous bookings were for tackles. But in Scotland his troubles come from protests. The game is so fast that referees and linesmen are late with decisions.'

St Johnstone receive the Pride of Perth Rosebowl.

The cup semi-final didn't escape controversy, but an unsighted referee could hardly be blamed for failing to spot a Tangerine clad arm deliberately deflecting a Maskrey shot. It was simply another indication that it wasn't to be Saints day. Even United international dynamo Jim McInally later confessed St Johnstone were the better side.

Totten revealed: 'The players were devastated. We were so near and yet so far that I think a 3-0 defeat would have been easier to accept. In the dressing room I told them we had forced nine corners to their five and 13 shots on goal compared with eight. I told them I couldn't have asked for any more effort than they gave me — Roddy Grant actually played on with a broken bone in his foot — then congratulated United and wished them well in the final.

'If I had it all to do tomorrow I think I would play exactly the same team. There were players on the bench that we'd paid £265,000 for but that doesn't matter to me. We'd spent £600 on Don McVicar and he was marvellous in that match. There are no favourites. It's all about a team effort at Perth. We share the good times and bad.

'I've been in football for 30 years and that defeat was the most painful of the lot. It was the most disappointing weekend of my life. It's every manager's dream to lead out his side in the cup final and I'm no different. It would have been the perfect end to an incredible season for St Johnstone.'

Six Premier matches were left on the programme and the cup blues were banished temporarily with victory over St Mirren securing the first home league bonus since Christmas. The poorest crowd of the season, at 3,295, reflected the disappointment felt through Perth and Kinross. But, overall, the revivalist movement nudged the average Perth attendance towards the 8,000 mark. Back in the Second Division days, had 23 home games really attracted just 27,000 customers?

Defeat by the ultimate champions at Ibrox — just days before Graeme Souness announced his defection to Liverpool — saw Lindsay Hamilton felled by Mark Hateley's Desperate Dan-like chin, prompting five stitches to a gaping head wound and an understudy role for Don McVicar; Hearts dispelled any lingering hopes of pilfering a European invite; and the curtain came down with one point to show from Hibs and single goal defeats by championship contenders Aberdeen and a Celtic side snatching a UEFA invitation, but dispensing with the services of their manager. With injuries and suspensions piling up, opportunities were extended for younger fringe players like winger David Bingham and defender Keith Nicolson to go through their paces.

The final league placings showed Saints at number seven, 12 points clear of bottom club St Mirren. Naturally, the fabulous exploits over the first half of the campaign had prompted even loftier ambitions, but Perth fans had to trek 20 years back down memory lane to recall the last occasion their side featured in such company.

'Had anyone predicted we would be sitting in fourth place and chasing a European spot via the league and cup into the month of March, they would have been laughed out of court at the start of the season,' said Totten. 'We beat every team in the league, with the exception of the champions, Rangers. The club attracted praise from all quarters and when I received the Manager of the Year award, it was also recognition for the efforts made by countless people in transforming St Johnstone Football Club.'

Accompanying Totten to the glamorous Glasgow awards ceremony was chairman Geoff Brown. Reflecting on five magical years, it seemed barely credible that a football club flirting with following Third Lanark into the history books had been revived and hailed officially as 'The Pride of Perth'.

Financially, the Fair City club was on a sounder footing than at any time in its history, with premises the envy of most British clubs. Success in football can be transitory, but a club which had once relied on gaming machines to pay the players' wages was no longer gambling with its very existence. A glance at the list of transfer deals spanning five years revealed that the club had invested more than £1 million in players, with no big money sales. But in terms of financial stability, it now had few rivals.

'Being hailed among Scotland's so-called Big Six was a real compliment to the club, but in terms of finance and stadia we're really in the top three. Unlike every other team in the United Kingdom, we aren't having to think about ground improvements. This club is in an enviable position.

'It's impossible to separate football from the business side of the club. The two strands are inextricably linked. We have achieved financial stability and while every effort will continue to be made to improve the quality of the playing staff, that stability will not be placed in jeopardy in the transfer market. Our philosophy hasn't changed since the days when we were the 38th club in Scotland.

'People ask where St Johnstone go from here,' concluded Brown. 'All my life I've believed in setting a realistic target and trying to reach it. Having achieved that it's simply time to raise the sights that little bit higher. There are no guarantees and we make no promises. But believe me, everyone at McDiarmid Park harbours even greater ambitions for this club.'

Facts and Figures

Appearances 1986/87

	Substitute	League	Scottish Cup	Skol Cup	Total Starts
Sammy Johnston	1	38	3	2	43
Ken Wilson	1	38	3	2	43
Willie Brown	—	35	3	2	40
Doug Barron	1	35	3	2	40
Gordon Winter	2	34	2	2	38
Ian Gibson	—	30	3	2	35
Andy Millen	3	30	3	2	35
John Balavage	—	26	3	2	31
Davie Lloyd	2	23	3	—	26
Don McVicar	—	23	3	—	26
Ian Heddle	—	19	3	—	22
Willie Watson	5	21	—	—	21
Graeme Payne	16	17	1	—	18
Derek McKay	4	12	—	1	13
Gordon Henderson	—	8	—	—	8
Joe McGurn	6	6	—	1	7
Charlie Adam	1	5	—	2	7
Joe Ward	13	5	—	1	6
George Watson	—	5	—	—	5
Pat Barkey	11	4	—	1	5
Gerry Crawley	1	3	—	—	3
Scott Douglas	3	3	—	—	3
Jim Bowie	1	2	—	—	2
Craig Mailer	1	2	—	—	2
Mike Smith	3	2	—	—	2
Paul Hannigan	—	1	—	—	1
Kevin Thoms	3	1	—	—	1
Martin Duffy	1	—	—	—	—
Robert Green	3	—	—	—	—
Gary Maher	1	—	—	—	—

Appearances 1987/88

	Substitute	League	Scottish Cup	Skol Cup	Total Starts
Doug Barron	—	38	4	3	45
Alan McKillop	—	38	4	3	45
Sammy Johnston	1	38	4	3	45
John Balavage	—	37	4	3	44
Tommy Coyle	1	38	4	2	44
Don McVicar	1	38	2	3	43
Ian Heddle	1	35	4	3	42
Ken Thomson	—	35	4	—	39
Steve Maskrey	6	28	2	3	33
Gary Thompson	3	26	4	—	30
Willie Watters	6	18	4	—	22
Willie Brown	1	12	—	3	15
Joe McGurn	12	11	—	3	14
Danny Powell	10	10	2	—	12
Mike Smith	16	9	2	—	11
Grant Jenkins	8	8	—	—	8
Ken Wilson	4	3	—	3	6
Steve Gavin	13	3	—	—	3
Jim Butter	—	2	—	—	2
Davie Lloyd	6	—	—	1	1
Keith Nicolson	—	1	—	—	1
Craig Mailer	3	—	—	—	—

Appearances 1988/89

	Substitute	League	Scottish Cup	Skol Cup	Total Starts
John Balavage	—	39	6	1	46
Doug Barron	—	38	6	1	45
Paul Cherry	4	36	6	—	42
Ian Heddle	1	35	5	1	41
Ken Thomson	—	33	6	1	40
Steve Maskrey	—	31	5	1	37
Don McVicar	—	28	6	1	35
Gary Thompson	—	30	3	1	34
Roddy Grant	—	28	6	—	34
Tommy Coyle	8	25	5	1	31
Grant Jenkins	11	24	4	—	28
Stuart Sorbie	15	24	2	1	27
Sammy Johnston	11	21	4	—	25
John Irvine	11	8	2	—	10
Willie Watters	9	7	—	1	8
Mike Smith	8	7	—	—	7
Alan McKillop	—	3	—	1	4
Keith Nicolson	2	3	—	—	3
Mark Treanor	—	3	—	—	3
Gary Maher	1	2	—	—	2
David Martin	2	1	—	—	1
Willie Newbigging	—	1	—	—	1
Billy Spence	9	1	—	—	1

Appearances 1989/90

	Substitute	League	Scottish Cup	Skol Cup	Total Starts
John Balavage	—	38	1	1	40
Paul Cherry	1	38	1	1	40
Don McVicar	—	35	1	1	37
Ian Heddle	1	34	1	1	36
Sammy Johnston	4	34	1	1	36
Allan Moore	—	33	1	1	35
Roddy Grant	6	33	—	—	33
Mark Treanor	—	30	—	—	30
Harry Curran	8	26	1	1	28
Ken Thomson	1	24	1	1	26
Steve Maskrey	7	22	1	—	23
Grant Jenkins	9	20	—	1	21
Doug Barron	4	16	1	—	17
Paul Hegarty	—	14	—	—	14
Gary McGinnis	1	10	—	—	10
Kenny Ward	17	6	—	—	6
Alan McKillop	—	5	—	—	5
Billy Blackie	9	2	1	—	3
Willie Newbigging	—	1	—	1	2
Gary Thompson	5	1	—	1	2
David Bingham	—	1	—	—	1
Jim Butter	—	1	—	—	1
Keith Nicolson	—	1	—	—	1
Mike Smith	5	—	—	—	—
Stuart Sorbie	2	—	—	—	—
Gary Maher	1	—	—	—	—

Appearances 1990/91

	Substitute	League	Scottish Cup	Skol Cup	Total Starts
Harry Curran	—	35	5	1	41
Sergei Baltacha	—	34	5	1	40
Lindsay Hamilton	—	34	5	—	39
Gary McGinnis	—	32	5	1	38
Steve Maskrey	1	33	5	—	38
Allan Moore	—	31	5	1	37
Mark Treanor	—	30	5	1	36
John Inglis	—	31	4	1	36
Roddy Grant	3	29	4	1	34
Tommy Turner	1	26	5	—	31
Don McVicar	8	18	4	1	23
Paul Cherry	4	18	—	—	18
John Davies	11	13	2	—	15
Paul Sweeney	2	8	—	—	8
Kenny MacDonald	8	5	1	—	6
David Bingham	3	4	—	1	5
Keith Nicolson	—	5	—	—	5
John Balavage	—	2	—	1	3
Doug Barron	10	3	—	—	3
Ian Heddle	8	3	—	—	3
Sammy Johnston	1	—	—	1	1
Iain Lee	7	1	—	—	1
Kenny Ward	16	1	—	—	1
Paul Deas	1	—	—	—	—

Goalscorers 1986/87

	League	Scottish Cup	Skol Cup	Total
Willie Brown	24	4	—	28
Sammy Johnston	6	1	—	7
Derek McKay	7	—	—	7
Davie Lloyd	5	1	—	6
Graeme Payne	5	—	—	5
Ian Gibson	3	1	—	4
Ian Heddle	3	—	—	3
Don McVicar	2	1	—	3
Andy Millen	1	1	—	2
Charlie Adam	—	—	1	1
Joe Ward	1	—	—	1
Gordon Winter	1	—	—	1

Goalscorers 1987/88

	League	Scottish Cup	Skol Cup	Total
Willie Watters	16	2	—	18
Sammy Johnston	11	2	1	14
Tommy Coyle	13	—	—	13
Ian Heddle	9	—	1	10
Alan McKillop	5	1	1	7
Steve Maskrey	5	1	—	6
Willie Brown	3	—	2	5
Danny Powell	3	2	—	5
Mike Smith	2	—	—	2
Doug Barron	1	—	—	1
Steve Gavin	1	—	—	1
Grant Jenkins	1	—	—	1
Davie Lloyd	1	—	—	1
Don McVicar	1	—	—	1
Gary Thompson	1	—	—	1
Ken Thomson	1	—	—	1

Goalscorers 1988/89

	League	Scottish Cup	Skol Cup	Total
Steve Maskrey	11	4	—	15
Grant Jenkins	10	1	—	11
Stuart Sorbie	7	1	—	8
Roddy Grant	4	1	—	5
Willie Watters	4	—	—	4
Ian Heddle	2	1	—	3
Sammy Johnston	3	—	—	3
Tommy Coyle	2	1	—	3
Don McVicar	3	—	—	3
Paul Cherry	2	—	—	2

Goalscorers 1989/90

	League	Scottish Cup	Skol Cup	Total
Roddy Grant	19	—	—	19
Allan Moore	13	—	—	13
Steve Maskrey	12	—	—	12
Sammy Johnston	7	—	—	7
Ian Heddle	5	—	—	5
Paul Cherry	4	—	—	4
Kenny Ward	4	—	—	4
Don McVicar	3	—	—	3
Harry Curran	3	—	—	3
Grant Jenkins	3	—	—	3
Mark Treanor	3	—	—	3
Paul Hegarty	1	—	—	1

Goalscorers 1990/91

	League	Scottish Cup	Skol Cup	Total
Harry Curran	9	2	—	11
Steve Maskrey	7	3	—	10
Allan Moore	5	4	—	9
Roddy Grant	7	2	—	9
Mark Treanor	4	—	—	4
Tommy Turner	3	—	—	3
David Bingham	2	—	—	2
John Davies	1	—	—	1
John Inglis	1	—	—	1
Don McVicar	1	—	—	1
Kenny Ward	1	—	—	1

Results 1986/87

(St Johnstone scores first)

DIVISION TWO

	Home		Away	
Meadowbank	1-5		1-1,	1-2
East Stirling	3-0		1-1,	2-0
Albion Rovers	1-2		2-0,	4-3
Stirling Albion	2-1		0-1,	1-1
Cowdenbeath	1-0,	1-0	3-4	
Arbroath	2-0		1-1,	4-1
Alloa Athletic	1-3,	2-1	3-3	
Queen's Park	3-0,	0-2	0-0	
Stranraer	0-3,	0-1	1-1	
Raith Rovers	1-1		2-2,	1-1
Berwick Rangers	3-2,	2-0	2-1	
Stenhousemuir	1-0,	0-1	1-1	
Ayr United	2-2		2-0,	1-1

SKOL CUP

	Home	Away
Cowdenbeath (1st Round)		1-0
Clydebank (2nd Round)		0-3

SCOTTISH CUP

	Home	Away
Queen's Park (2nd Round)	4-1	
Whitehill Welfare (3rd Round)	4-0	
Forfar Athletic (4th Round)	1-2	

Results 1987/88

(St Johnstone scores first)

DIVISION TWO

	Home		Away	
Ayr United	0-0,	2-0	3-0	
Cowdenbeath	0-1		3-0,	0-1
Brechin City	1-1,	2-0	1-2	
Arbroath	3-1,	4-0	2-0	
Stenhousemuir	4-1		0-0,	0-3
Stranraer	1-0		2-1,	3-1
Queen's Park	2-0,	1-2	1-0	
Stirling Albion	1-1,	1-0	6-0	
East Stirling	3-1,	0-0	2-0	
Alloa Athletic	2-1		1-1,	1-1
Berwick Rangers	2-1		4-0,	2-0
Montrose	1-1,	5-1	1-0	
Albion Rovers	4-1,	2-0	1-1	

SKOL CUP

	Home	Away
Alloa (1st Round)	4-1	
St Mirren (2nd Round)		1-0
Aberdeen (3rd Round)		0-3

SCOTTISH CUP

	Home	Away
Albion Rovers (1st Round)		1-1
Albion Rovers (Replay)	2-0	
Fraserburgh (2nd Round)		5-2
Aberdeen (3rd Round)	0-1	

Results 1988/89

(St Johnstone scores first)

DIVISION ONE

	Home		Away	
Raith Rovers	3-1		1-1,	2-0
Dunfermline Athletic	0-1		0-1,	0-1
Forfar Athletic	2-1		1-1,	1-1
Airdrie	2-1,	1-1	0-1	
Morton	4-2,	0-1	1-1	
Meadowbank Thistle	0-0		1-1,	1-2
Ayr United	2-0,	0-1	1-2	
Partick Thistle	2-1,	1-1	0-2	
Falkirk	2-1,	0-1	1-2	
Queen of the South	3-1,	3-1	1-1	
Clyde	0-0		4-2,	0-2
Kilmarnock	2-0,	2-2	3-0	
Clydebank	2-0		0-2,	2-2

SKOL CUP

		Away
Hearts (2nd Round)		0-5

SCOTTISH CUP

	Home	Away
Stenhousemuir (3rd Round)	2-0	
Forfar Athletic (4th Round)	2-1	
Morton (5th Round)		2-2
Morton (Replay)	3-2	
Rangers (Semi Final)		0-0
Rangers (Replay)		0-4

(Both matches played at Celtic Park)

Results 1989/90

(St Johnstone scores first)

DIVISION ONE

	Home		Away	
Alloa Athletic	3-0,	6-0	1-0	
Clydebank	2-1,	1-3	0-4	
Forfar Athletic	3-1,	1-0	5-1	
Raith Rovers	1-2,	0-0	2-0	
Hamilton Accies	3-0		3-3,	3-2
Albion Rovers	2-1		3-1,	5-2
Airdrie	1-2,	3-1	2-2	
Falkirk	2-0		3-3,	0-1
Meadowbank Thistle	1-0,	1-2	3-1	
Morton	1-1		0-0,	2-1
Clyde	2-0,	1-1	2-0	
Ayr United	4-0		2-2,	2-0
Partick Thistle	2-1		1-0,	2-0

SKOL CUP

		Away
Queen of the South (2nd Round)		0-1

SCOTTISH CUP

		Away
Rangers (3rd Round)		0-3

Results 1990/91
(St Johnstone scores first)

PREMIER LEAGUE

	Home		Away	
Dundee United	1-3,	0-1	2-1,	0-0
St Mirren	0-1,	2-1	2-2,	1-0
Motherwell	2-1,	1-4	0-3,	2-2
Dunfermline Athletic	3-2,	0-1	2-1,	2-3
Hibernian	1-1,	0-0	0-1,	1-0
Aberdeen	5-0,	0-1	0-0,	1-2
Celtic	3-2,	2-3	0-0,	0-3
Hearts	2-1,	0-2	3-2,	1-2
Rangers	0-0,	1-1	1-4,	0-3

SKOL CUP

Clyde (2nd Round)	0-2

SCOTTISH CUP

Berwick Rangers (3rd Round)	0-0	
Berwick Rangers (Replay)		4-3 (a.e.t.)
Hibernian (4th Round)	2-1	
Ayr United (5th Round)	5-2	
Dundee United (Semi Final)	1-2	
	(East End Park)	

Final Table 1986/87

DIVISION TWO

	P	W	D	L	F	A	Pts
Meadowbank Thistle	39	23	9	7	69	38	55
Raith Rovers	39	16	20	3	73	44	52
Stirling Albion	39	20	12	7	55	33	52
Ayr United	39	22	8	9	70	49	52
St Johnstone	**39**	**16**	**13**	**10**	**59**	**49**	**45**
Alloa	39	17	7	15	48	50	41
Cowdenbeath	39	16	8	15	59	55	40
Albion Rovers	39	15	9	15	48	51	39
Queen's Park	39	9	19	11	48	49	37
Stranraer	39	9	11	19	41	59	29
Arbroath	39	11	7	21	46	66	29
Stenhousemuir	39	10	9	20	37	58	29
East Stirling	39	6	11	22	33	56	23
Berwick Rangers	39	8	7	24	40	69	23

Final Table 1987/88

DIVISION TWO

	P	W	D	L	F	A	Pts
Ayr United	39	27	7	5	95	31	61
St Johnstone	**39**	**25**	**9**	**5**	**74**	**24**	**59**
Queen's Park	39	21	9	9	64	44	51
Brechin City	39	20	8	11	56	40	48
Stirling Albion	39	18	10	11	60	51	46
East Stirling	39	15	13	11	51	47	43
Alloa	39	16	8	15	50	46	40
Montrose	39	12	11	16	45	51	35
Arbroath	39	10	14	15	54	66	34
Stenhousemuir	39	12	9	18	49	58	33
Cowdenbeath	39	10	13	16	51	66	33
Albion Rovers	39	10	11	18	45	75	31
Berwick Rangers	39	6	4	29	32	77	16
Stranraer	39	4	8	27	34	84	16

Final Table 1988/89

DIVISION ONE

	P	W	D	L	F	A	Pts
Dunfermline Athletic	39	22	10	7	60	36	54
Falkirk	39	22	8	9	71	37	52
Clydebank	39	18	12	9	80	55	48
Airdrieonians	39	17	13	9	66	44	47
Morton	39	16	9	14	46	46	41
St Johnstone	**39**	**14**	**12**	**13**	**51**	**42**	**40**
Raith Rovers	39	15	10	14	50	52	40
Partick Thistle	39	13	11	15	57	58	37
Forfar Athletic	39	10	16	13	52	56	36
Meadowbank Thistle	39	13	10	16	45	50	36
Ayr United	39	13	9	17	56	72	35
Clyde	39	9	16	14	40	52	34
Kilmarnock	39	10	14	15	47	60	34
Queen of the South*	39	2	8	29	38	99	10

* *2 points deducted for breach of rules*

Final Table 1989/90

DIVISION ONE

	P	W	D	L	F	A	Pts
St Johnstone	**39**	**25**	**8**	**6**	**81**	**39**	**58**
Airdrie	39	23	8	8	77	45	54
Clydebank	39	17	10	12	74	64	44
Falkirk	39	14	15	10	59	46	43
Raith Rovers	39	15	12	12	57	50	42
Hamilton	39	14	13	12	52	53	41
Meadowbank	39	13	13	13	41	46	39
Partick Thistle	39	12	14	13	62	53	38
Clyde	39	10	15	14	39	46	35
Ayr United	39	11	13	15	41	62	35
Morton	39	9	16	14	38	46	34
Forfar*	39	8	15	16	51	65	29
Albion Rovers	39	8	11	20	50	78	27
Alloa	39	6	13	20	41	70	25

* 2 points deducted for breach of rules

Saints Alive!

Final Table 1990/91

PREMIER DIVISION

	P	W	D	L	F	A	Pts
Rangers	36	24	7	5	62	23	55
Aberdeen	36	22	9	5	62	27	53
Celtic	36	17	7	12	52	38	41
Dundee United	36	17	7	12	41	29	41
Hearts	36	14	7	15	48	55	35
Motherwell	36	12	9	15	51	50	33
St Johnstone	**36**	**11**	**9**	**16**	**41**	**54**	**31**
Dunfermline	36	8	11	17	38	61	27
Hibernian	36	6	13	17	24	51	25
St Mirren	36	5	9	22	28	59	19